Matthias Vodička

**Guideline for
the Development of Chinese Suppliers**

Matthias Vodička

Guideline for the Development of Chinese Suppliers

Improving the Buyer Supplier Relationship Using the Balanced Scorecard

VDM Verlag Dr. Müller

Bibliografische Information der Deutschen Nationalbibliothek:
Die Deutsche Nationalbibliothek verzeichnet diese Publikation in der Deutschen
Nationalbibliografie; detaillierte bibliografische Daten sind im Internet über
http://dnb.d-nb.de abrufbar.

Das Werk ist einschließlich aller seiner Teile urheberrechtlich geschützt. Jede
Verwertung außerhalb der engen Grenzen des Urheberrechtsgesetzes ist ohne
Zustimmung des Verlages unzulässig und strafbar. Das gilt insbesondere für
Vervielfältigungen, Übersetzungen, Mikroverfilmungen und die Einspeicherung
und Verarbeitung in elektronischen Systemen.

Alle in diesem Buch genannten Marken und Produktnamen unterliegen waren-
zeichen-, marken- oder patentrechtlichem Schutz bzw. sind Warenzeichen oder
eingetragene Warenzeichen der jeweiligen Inhaber. Die Wiedergabe von Marken,
Produktnamen, Gebrauchsnamen, Handelsnamen, Warenbezeichnungen u.s.w. in
diesem Werk berechtigt auch ohne besondere Kennzeichnung nicht zu der
Annahme, dass solche Namen im Sinne der Warenzeichen- und Markenschutz-
gesetzgebung als frei zu betrachten wären und daher von jedermann benutzt
werden dürften.

Copyright © 2007 VDM Verlag Dr. Müller e. K. und Lizenzgeber
Alle Rechte vorbehalten. Saarbrücken 2007
Kontakt: VDM Verlag Dr. Müller e.K., Dudweiler Landstr. 125 a,
D-66123 Saarbrücken, Telefon 0681/9100-698, Telefax 0180 5060 3388 4322,
Email: info@vdm-verlag.de
Coverbild: www.purestockx.com
Covererstellung: Britta Dietrich

Herstellung:
Schaltungsdienst Lange o.H.G., Zehrensdorfer Str. 11, D-12277 Berlin
Books on Demand GmbH, Gutenbergring 53, D-22848 Norderstedt

ISBN: 978-3-8364-0732-8

This work is the result of cooperation between

wbk – Institute for Production Science, University of Karlsruhe (TH), supervision by Prof. Jürgen Fleischer

and

AMI – Advanced Manufacturing Institute, Hong Kong University of Science and Technology, supervision by Prof. Mitchell M Tseng.

Supported with funds from the

Dr.-Ing. Willy-Höfler-Stiftung, Karlsruhe, Germany

Acknowledgements

Here, I would like to express my gratitude towards the many people, who supported this thesis professionally and personally, or inspired me in any other way. This list is not complete, so I would also like to thank everyone, who is not mentioned in the following, but is somehow connected to this work and my person.

In the first place I would like to thank Prof. Jürgen Fleischer, whose trust and support facilitated to work on this interesting topic at the marvelous University of Science and Technology in Hong Kong. Marc Wawerla earns many thanks for being a tolerant, always motivating and amicable supervisor - meeting in Shanghai and Hangzhou strengthened me a lot! Thanks also to Anna Lena Wagner, who co worked with me on a related topic and was always ready for fast feedback and support with relevant material.

Big gratitude earn all the students at the Advanced Manufacturing Institute, who affiliated me quickly into the AMI-family and eased the settling down at the HKUST. The small chats and the presentations gave me a lot of inspiration. Prof. Tseng, as head of the AMI, has to receive special thanks for the friendly invitation to his institute, and even more for his fair comments, strong personal involvement and high claims for meaningfulness and clearness. I got highly impressed by him as supervisor and mentor, also on a personal level. Thanks also for giving me the opportunity to spend time at the Zhejiang AMI in Hangzhou, where I could gather a lot of experiences about life in China within a very friendly environment. Further, it made possible to meet executives for interviews, who were willing to share their knowledge and hence, supported this thesis' practical relevancy to a great part; many thanks to the participants.

Further, I owe personal thanks to many of my fellow students, who were willing, patient and supportive, when listening to, and giving feedback on my thoughts, or supported this work by offering their precious time for review, like Amelie, Maxime, Michael and Rayan. Within this group, special thanks deserves my "co-co-supervisor" Felix Papier, who did not hesitate to spend many hours sharing his knowledge on scientific works, giving critical feedback and stimulating many ideas; this always encouraged me.

Last, thanks to my closest ones. Juemin, no matter how the wind of change blows, thank you for supporting my thought, to go to China. You inspired me to wish more and I believe I can achieve higher aims now. Further, high gratefulness is to be dedicated to my brothers David and Stephan, who one and the other were able to make me laugh over a distance of about 10 thousand kilometers, and so, gave me moments of feeling like home. And eventually, my greatest thanks are devoted to my mother and my father, whose interest was always to support, to motivate and to share, and who always smoothened the way for my valuable education and my life. *Mamí a tatí, děkuji Vám za Vaší věčnou a nekonečnou lásku.*

Thank you all, for giving me this unforgettable experience at my study's ending.

Matthias Vodicka, Hong Kong

Table of content

1 INTRODUCTION 1
   1.1 Motivation 1
   1.2 Objective 1
   1.3 Work structure 2

2 BASICS 4
   2.1 Definitions for this work 4
      2.1.1 Buyer and Supplier 4
      2.1.2 Supplier Development 4
      2.1.3 Supplier Improvement 4
      2.1.4 Supplier's capabilities 5
      2.1.5 Low Cost Country 5
   2.2 Supply chain management 5
   2.3 Procurement 5
      2.3.1 Performance Indicators 6
      2.3.2 Performance Measurement 7
      2.3.3 Supplier Management 8
      2.3.4 Supplier Controlling 9
      2.3.5 Supplier's Capabilities 9
   2.4 Global sourcing 10
      2.4.1 Low-cost sources in global procurement 10
      2.4.2 Considerations for Sourcing in China 11
      2.4.3 Procurement Activities in China 12
      2.4.4 Differences between markets 13
      2.4.5 China specific issues 14
      2.4.6 Differences in aims and company culture in ICs and China 16
   2.5 The Balanced Scorecard 17
      2.5.1 General framework 17
      2.5.2 Strategy maps 18
      2.5.3 Key Performance Indicators / Measures 19

3 STATE OF THE ART IN RESEARCH 21
   3.1 Supplier Development and Improvement 21
      3.1.1 Supplier Development 21

3.1.2	Supplier Development in China	24
3.1.3	Risk Assessment as part of the SD in China	28
3.1.4	Supplier Improvement as part of the supplier development	32
3.1.5	Supplier Improvement in China	36
3.2	Adapted BSCs for the Supply Chain Management	37
3.2.1	Description of approaches	37
3.2.2	Deficits for improvement in China	39

4 TODAY'S ISSUES AND PRACTICES OF THE INDUSTRY'S SUPPLIER DEVELOPMENT IN CHINA — **41**

4.1	Interviews with global playing companies in Germany	41
4.1.1	Target definition	41
4.1.2	Structure of the interview guideline	41
4.1.3	Results	42
4.2	Interviews with global playing companies in China	42
4.2.1	Target definition	42
4.2.2	Structure of the interview guideline	43
4.2.3	Three case studies	43
4.2.4	Results	46
4.3	Survey in Germany	47
4.4	Requirements for BS-Relationship Improvement in China	47

5 REQUIREMENTS FOR THE BSC APPROACH IN BRIEF — **49**

6 BSC-BASED RELATIONSHIP IMPROVEMENT AS PART OF THE SUPPLIER DEVELOPMENT IN CHINA — **50**

6.1	Adaptation of the BSC	51
6.1.1	Cooperation perspective	52
6.2	Improvement Strategy Maps	52
6.2.1	Strategy maps as roadmaps to improvement	53
6.2.2	Strategy map for Buyer Supplier Relationship Improvement	53
6.2.3	Strategy map for SI to meet minimum requirements	57
6.3	Improvement Balanced Scorecard	60
6.3.1	Buyer Supplier Relationship BSC	62
6.3.2	"Audit-BSC" to Boost Supplier's Capabilities	67
6.4	Organizational integration of the BSC	71

7 DISCUSSION — **73**

8   SUMMARY AND OUTLOOK **76**
    8.1 Summary   76
    8.2 Outlook   77
A.   REFERENCES   **I**
ANNEX   **IV**

Table of Figures

FIGURE 2.1 OUTSOURCING MAKES PROCUREMENT A KEY FUNCTION (/SOE-99/)	6
FIGURE 2.2 PERFORMANCE MEASUREMENT - REWARD SUPPLIER AND STAFF (/SOE-99/)	7
FIGURE 2.3 SUPPLIER MATURITY CURVE (/HAN-99/ P. 32)	10
FIGURE 2.4 PROCUREMENT ACTIVITIES PERFORMED AT DIFFERENT LEVELS (/SOE-99/)	12
FIGURE 2.5 INCREASE OF AVERAGE SOURCING QUOTA IN THE WORLD BY 2010	14
FIGURE 2.6 GRAPH SHOWING THE MAJOR PROBLEMS OCCURRING	14
ILLUSTRATION 2.7: FEW SUPPLIERS SEEM CAPABLE OF FULFILLING REQUIREMENTS	15
FIGURE 2.8 EMERGING CRITICAL RISKS DURING PROCUREMENT IN CHINA	16
FIGURE 2.9 A TEMPLATE BALANCED SCORECARD (CP. /CRE-05/)	18
FIGURE 2.10 FROM VISION TO STRATEGY MAP TO BALANCED SCORECARD	19
FIGURE 3.1 SUPPLIER DEVELOPMENT PROCESS (/DUN-04/)	21
FIGURE 3.2 PHASE 1: CONSTRAINTS (/DUN-04/)	21
FIGURE 3.3 PHASE 2: SPECIFICATIONS AND REQUIREMENTS (/DUN-04/)	22
FIGURE 3.4 PHASE 3: THE RELATIONSHIP AND THE NEEDS (/DUN-04/)	22
FIGURE 3.5 SUPPLIER DEVELOPMENT PROCESS (/FLE-06/)	24
FIGURE 3.6 INFORMATION SOURCES FOR SUPPLIER IDENTIFICATION (/WAG-06/)	25
FIGURE 3.7 ASSESSMENT TOOL WITH CRITERIA AT DIFFERENT LEVELS (/WAG-06/)	26
FIGURE 3.8 STEPS OF THE RISK-FMEA (/FLE-06/)	30
FIGURE 3.9 RISK HEIGHT (/FLE-06/)	31
FIGURE 3.10 RISK MAP (/FLE-06/)	31
FIGURE 3.11 SUPPLIER DEVELOPMENT (/KRA-99/)	33
FIGURE 3.12 GRAPH SHOWING THE IMPORTANCE OF BUSINESS AREAS TO FOCUS	36
FIGURE 3.13 SCM FRAMEWORK ALIGNED TO THE BSC PERSPECTIVES (/RUG-06/)	38
FIGURE 6.1 BSC BASED BUYER SUPPLIER RELATIONSHIP IMPROVEMENT	51
FIGURE 6.2 ILLUSTRATION PROCESS TO PROJECTPLAN FOR IMPROVEMENT	53
FIGURE 6.3 BUYER SUPPLIER RELATIONSHIP IMPROVEMENT STRATEGY MAP (THEMES)	54

FIGURE 6.4 TEMPLATE STRATEGY MAP FOR A HOLISTIC CAPABILITY IMPROVEMENT   58

FIGURE 6.5 THEME-A-BSC OF THE RELATIONSHIP IMPROVEMENT BSC   63

FIGURE 6.6 IMPROVEMENT COMPONENTS FROM ASSESSMENTS AND PRODUCT SPECS   68

FIGURE 6.7 ILLUSTRATION OF FINDING IMPROVEMENT COMPONENTS   69

1 Introduction

1.1 Motivation

Nowadays companies all over the world face global competition. To stay competitive, procurement developed to be a major leverage to save cost in the recent years. As part of it, the supplier management is increasingly considered to be an important business function. Further, the development of supply bases in low-cost-countries (LCC), as China is, over the past years rapidly gained significance. After years of mass production of mostly simple products in China, today Industrialized-Country (IC) companies from the mechanical engineering industry strive for the sourcing of bought-in parts from Chinese suppliers.

IC companies penetrating the Chinese market with the target to source locally have to develop a supply base first. The supplier development identifies the required suppliers, assesses them upon their capabilities and establishes a co-operation. A successful supply needs supplier improvement, since fundamental capabilities are lacking frequently. Further, risks weigh heavier due to the high investments required in advance. Considering mainly small and medium sized enterprises in investment goods industry, the regular problems in China are enlarged by low purchasing volumes and specialized products. These companies face Chinese suppliers with lacking commitment to quality and delivery in time, which represent fundamental problems. Further barriers to supplier improvement emerge from the differing culture and the supplier's strategic orientation. Therefore, a new approach considering the local issues and risks is suggested in order to enhance the benefits from the executed efforts.

1.2 Objective

In the scope of this work, the existing methods and concepts of supplier-development and supplier improvement, which are applied in Industrialized Countries and in China, have to be investigated and presented. This investigation has to include both desktop research and information from companies that are involved in China sourcing in order to increase the practical relevancy. The specific aspects of business relationships in China have to be shown and the main barriers pointed out, as well, as possibilities emerging. With these facts as basis, a new concept has to be worked out, which provides enhancement to the existing methods of supplier capability improvement by considering the local requirements for a prosperous buyer supplier relationship in China.

The supplier development as process of developing a new supply base has to be analyzed showing the general occurring issues and prospects of buyer's supplier development effort, and be weighed upon its relevancy in China. The supplier improvement with preliminary steps, as it is a key process of the supplier development in China, has to be emphasized and analyzed upon its applicability with Chinese suppliers. From that, the elementary steps to undertake and the main deficits for China have to be identified. Based on the found requirements in China and the deficits of common methods a new approach has to be designed. This approach is based on the Balanced Scorecard (BSC) and has to be applicable to improve the relationship, between the IC buyer and the Chinese supplier, itself. Aligning the companies' differing strategies, the BSC shows a possible way to improvement, resulting in both parties' benefits. Within this relationship improvement, the supplier's deficient capabilities have to be focused, since they are responsible for the major risks for both companies; thereagainst, the buyer's efforts have to regard the Chinese culture and needs, in order to be successful with his undertaking. Expected results of BSC-based relationship improvement are mutual trust, commitment and enhanced communication, leading to a fast improvement and a prosperous relationship for both companies.

1.3 Work structure

In order to attain meaningful results, this work's approach is based on recent research and on a survey on today's industry's issues, practices and benefits in China. In the beginning of this work, definitions are given on the main terms required. So e.g. supplier development and improvement may be confused, since these terms may not be differentiated in other works. Further, explanations are given to show the constraints and the considered aspects. After that, the changes of supply chain management in the last years, and the emerging issues are discussed in order to show the basic need for an enhanced approach.

In the following, the supplier management is focused. The fundamental circumstances to consider are discussed and beneficial practices shown. The supplier management involves a performance measurement system for both supplier and procurement department. The supplier controlling can be of strategic and operative nature. The basics on performance indicators are introduced and an illustration on the meaning of the supplier's capabilities maturity is given. This is followed by a discussion about global sourcing that brings in chances and risks. Low cost country sourcing contains special characteristics, so the sourcing in China is focused and drivers for success are shown. Presenting the main procurement activities and their application in China, the supplier development and improvement in China with its goals are focused. In order to understand the importance for a structured approach, the differences between the IC and Chinese market are shown and the specific occurring issues analyzed. This is concluded by the differences in aims and company culture between IC and Chinese companies. Last in this chapter, the Balanced Scorecard is presented as it is the method of choice for the later approach. The aim and the measures of the BSC are explained. Further, the strategy maps are a useful extension of the BSC, so they are introduced as well.

In chapter 3 researches on supplier development are discussed, the general issues presented and evaluated upon applicability in China. A recent approach on supplier development for China is presented, which represents a guideline for the development of a Chinese supply base. It also considers the required steps for supplier improvement. The risk assessment plays an essential role in supplier development, so it is emphasized and conclusions for the supplier improvement derived. Further, the supplier improvement approaches in research are discussed. They show the major drivers for success and the possible barriers. These factors have to be considered in the approach to design. The second part of the desktop research deals with the current Balanced Scorecard approaches suggesting using the BSC in an inter-organizational environment. From latter ones beneficial elements can be extracted for the later approach.

In chapter 4 the survey results are presented. Beginning with interviews conducted in Germany, the structure of the interview guideline is described; interest is given to the companies' aims followed by their China sourcing activity. Emphasis lies on supplier assessment and improvement. After the description of results, the interviews with China located companies are presented. These interviews aim to identify the triggers of supplier improvement activities and the experiences made. Further, the expectations, the practices and the most critical elements are relevant. Three case studies illustrate experiences of companies differing in size, strategies and products. This is followed by results that are derived from the information given. The data attained from the survey confirms partially desktop research findings, but also uncovers elementary requirements for the improvement in China.

Chapter 5 shows the most important findings from desktop research and interviews briefly. Thus, based on other approaches' deficits, the room for research is found. Suggestions for the design of the buyer supplier relationship BSC are given.

In the beginning of chapter 6 the required adaptation of the Balanced Scorecard is explained. The cooperation perspective is added to enable the alignment of the two strongly differing companies' strategies. To enhance communication and understanding the strategy map is found to be a useful tool. It shows the cause and effects of strategic objectives and it helps the supplier and the buyer to comprehend the requirements. The on the previous findings based strategy maps are divided into two categories: (1) the buyer supplier relationship improvement includes the required objectives leading to both companies benefits; (2) the "Audit-Strategy Map" includes the required steps to undertake in order to reach the minimum level of requirements. Next, the Balanced Scorecards are presented. Aligned to the Strategy Maps they follow the given cause and effect, and provide a framework to measure and steer the tangible and intangible assets of the given buyer supplier relationship. With that a project plan can be set up, including targets, actions and responsibilities.

In chapter 7 the BSC approach is assessed upon its advantages, applicability and limitations within a buyer supplier relationship. A summary and an outlook for future research conclude this work.

2 Basics

2.1 Definitions for this work

2.1.1 Buyer and Supplier

The Industrialized Country (IC) company (buyer) concentrates on its core competencies in the investment goods industry; it sources specialized products in low volumes from suppliers in order to manufacture and deliver finalized products to an end-customer. The suppliers are the companies, which supply to the buyer. For this work's scope, these suppliers are local Chinese companies. In the discussion of literature however, suppliers are generally meant to be companies in Industrialized Countries.

2.1.2 Supplier Development

In this work, the supplier development is defined as the activities to execute in order to build up a new supply base. According to Dunn (/Dun-04/), it may be in other works defined as the actions to undertake in order to improve a supplier's business process to achieve a better supplier performance or enhance his capabilities. However, since this work includes both of these processes, supplier improvement and supplier development need to be clearly differentiated. The supplier development represents the process to develop a supply base: starting with the identification of the parts to source and ending with the termination of the relationship. Latter is due to the fact that the continuous supplier improvement and management are both considered to be part of the supplier development process. In cases of another definition of the term "supplier development" in examined literature, an adaptation to this work's definitions was conducted to avoid confusion (this counts for cited passages as well).

2.1.3 Supplier Improvement

The supplier improvement is part of the supplier development process. Supplier improvement activities can range from a passive verbal or written request for improvement by the buyer, up to an active involvement with transfer of know how and buyer's employees involved at the supplier's site to improve supplier's capabilities.

Passive involvement is the traditional approach and commonly used in different industries: it is reactive in nature, so it bases on past performance indicators. Companies regularly assess the supplier performance upon foregoing orders' results, e.g. delivery delays, quality complaints, etc. A report is being worked out and discussed with the supplier. The supplier has to improve his performance over a given time, otherwise rejection impends to him. For passive involvement, the supplier has to be to a certain level dependent on the buyer. Otherwise, the threat of rejection would have no effect.

Active involvement is a newer approach, which has emerged in different industries in the 1990's. Since companies have increasingly to concentrate on their core-competencies, suppliers obtain higher responsibility in the supply chain, resulting in the buyers' higher dependency. This led to the concept of active supplier improvement. It means that the buyer supports the supplier to improve his capabilities: e.g. consulting him on certain processes, giving workshops, etc. It is mostly applied to fix problems on the short term to lever the supplier's capabilities so that the buyer's basic requirements are met.

2.1.4 Supplier's capabilities

The supplier's capabilities are basically the abilities to fulfill the buyer's requirements. Essentially, they are the production processes respectively all processes having impact on the supplied part. However, in this work it also includes the supplier's company culture, which has great impact on the relationship and for which the buyer also may have requirements (e.g. cooperation willingness, strategic orientation etc.).

2.1.5 Low Cost Country

Low Cost Countries are considered to be the countries, where production of goods is possible at lower cost, compared to Industrialized Countries. This effect is strong for developing countries, with low labor or material costs. The low cost naturally mustn't be taken as an absolute term. It refers to theoretically possible cost savings. In contrast, the risk and diverse other cost rise, lowering the savings, and, in some cases, even turning the savings into losses. In this work the emphasis lies on China. However, many characteristics and issues emerging on the Chinese market and from Chinese suppliers may be transferable to other developing countries, where sourcing at low cost can be possible.

2.2 Supply chain management

"The comprehensive definition of "Supply Chain Management" (SCM) is the coordination of material and information flow from raw material in the ground to the end-customers' recycling of the expired product" (/Had-04/). The Council of Supply Chain Management Professionals (CSCMP) defined that SCM "encompasses the planning and management of all activities involved in sourcing and procurement (…). Importantly, it also includes coordination and collaboration with channel partners, which can be suppliers (…) and customers. In essence, SCM integrates supply and demand management within and across companies" (/CSC-06/).

The changes in manufacturing have been revolutionary since the early 1990's. Quality and performance techniques for example ISO9000, Six Sigma, Baldrige, TQM among many others and the implementation of IT-systems like Resource Planning Systems, relationship management systems etc., supported businesses to lean their production, increase quality and lower prices. These changes have the aim of enhancing the supply chain; the results were satisfying. However, parallel effects emerged. On the one hand, buyers are more dependent on suppliers, so that effective sourcing and relationship management gained a considerable strategic importance in an organization. On the other hand, the strategic sourcing still emphasizes the performance indicators like quality, delivery and price. Latter ones do not sufficiently support the relationship improvement to a collaborative one (/Nee-04/ p. 34). Soellner and Mackrodt (/Soe-99 / p. 16) state that "for leading companies to have world-class procurement operations, the central focus of their procurement organization must be managing supplier relationships". Jehle (/Jeh-02/ p. 3) concludes that growing varieties and complexity of products and services require enhancements in product- and process-related competencies. At the same time, the rising world competition and cost situation lead to the companies' concentration on core competencies with present capacities. In this contradicting environment, the cooperation of organizations in production and logistics networks was identified as important success driver.

2.3 Procurement

As Soellner and Mackrodt (/Soe-99/) explain, the procurement department traditionally had the function to supply the company with the predetermined needs, whilst being responsible that the materials and services required were available at the lowest price. Latter was considered to be the best way to contribute to the company's success. Regarding the focus on core competencies, higher innovation potentials from the suppliers, and the optimization of management-efficiency, the importance of the supplier management increased strongly over the past years. The supply base is jointly responsible for the long term success (/Wag-03/). According to Soellner and Mackrodt, this has its root cause in the change the companies underlay in the last decades, when concentrations on core competencies led to an increase of outsourcing to suppliers (cp. Figure 2.1). The result is that procurement became a key factor for competitiveness (/Soe-99/).

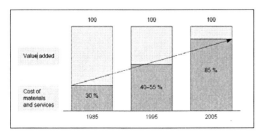

Figure 2.1 Outsourcing makes procurement a key function (/Soe-99/)

According to Handfield (/Han-02/ p. 15, et seq.) many companies still focus on single transactions and the orders settled, without aligning them to the other functions of the business, the suppliers or the customers. The organizations have to be able to compete, besides of on the basic factors like cost, quality, delivery and technology, on the basis of time, since companies have to be faster than the competition (/Han-02/ p. 38) (today time is also a big cost driver). However, the performance measurement focuses on overall supply chain effectiveness. This includes also the consideration of the customers and the suppliers.

Therefore, companies increasingly strive for the development of longer term relationships with key customers and suppliers and apply strategies for improvement and sharing of information between the parties. Handfield states that a key element of improved relationships is the application of an objective performance measurement system, with a mutual understanding of targets. To attain proper solutions, communication has to be fostered, clear objectives established and conflict causes avoided. On this basis, trust and further improvements can be achieved.

2.3.1 Performance Indicators

According to Terenzini (/Ter-94/ p. 11, et seq.), performance indicators (PI) can have different targets and characteristics, and underlie different objectives of appliance. However, the meaning of PIs can be stated briefly in "measures of how well something is being done". It is not fixed whether performance indicators have to be always quantitative measures or could also be qualitative ones. They can be used to show trends "performance indicators show trends in performance as opposed to current value or level of activity". This can provide a basis for strategic decisions that have impact on the future development. PIs are always connected to a certain goal with a specific direction (whereat the statistical tools give information without direct connection to a future action or objective). Further, Terenzini (/Ter-94/ p. 12, et seq.) explains that PIs simplify data by extracting some meaning of them and putting them into a describable context. In order to improve processes, the data attained has to be meaningful, so the values have to be normalized by another value or ratios created (/Ter-94/ p. 24, et seq.). From the measures monitored, the "health, effectiveness, and efficiency of an organization can be determined" (/Ter-94/ p. 64). Terenzini (/Ter-94/ p. 96) concludes that "performance indicators need to have a clear purpose, be coordinated throughout an organization or system (vertical alignment), extended across the entire range of organizational processes (horizontal alignment), be derived from a variety of coordinated methods, and be used to inform decision making." Neef (/Nee-04/ p. 163, et seq.) states that indicators need to be acceptable in the whole company, be clearly defined, and be reliable measures of criteria (direct connection and always measurable). In order to save resources, performance indicators have to be easy to measure and record. Neef states, in brief, performance indicators ought to be "SMART: specific, measurable, attainable, relevant, and time-framed".

As part of a decision making process in procurement, performance indicators are used for the supplier improvement. They show deficiencies and measure the progress of improvement. Handfield (/Han-99/ p. 28) suggests to measure besides of the conventional assessment criteria quality, delivery and costs ("while still important") other measures, missing for attaining the "whole picture": e.g. evidences for continuous improvement and efficiency, lead-time fulfillment and inventory risk reduction and others.

2.3.2 Performance Measurement

Wagner (/Wag-03/) explains the supplier management as process of "planning, implementing, developing, and monitoring company relationships with current and potential suppliers" or "organizing the optimal flow of (…) components to manufacturing companies from (…) suppliers". For both of these descriptions, the performance measurement is required, since "people can't manage what they can't measure, and they can't measure what they can't describe", (/Kap-04/ p. 3) the capabilities have always to be expressed in a particular way.

In the past the low price contracts, single orders and the supplier audits were the main contributions of the procurement. Today, the measures are different. Measures are connected to the value created by the procurement by having an incentive system for both procurement staff and supplier, since both are becoming processes with strategic relevancy. Following is explained as characteristics of the needed measurement system: "continuous, formal, objective, quantifiable, transparent and value-added oriented". In house and suppliers' contributions are distinguished regularly (Figure 2.1) (/Soe-99/ p. 19, et seq.).

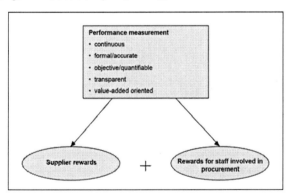

Figure 2.2 Performance measurement - reward supplier and staff (/Soe-99/)

For the supplier the contributions regarding the product innovation, the provided quality rates and the delivery on time are the main indicators. Further, the buyer's reaction can be measured, e.g. the returns, repairs and complaints on the products, giving information on the buyer's satisfaction. The buyer's procurement performance can be measured by the production relevant processes (cost of ownership, inventory levels etc.), the supplier structure with its characteristics (e.g. A-suppliers, internationality, brands etc.), the comparison of its own solutions to the competitors, and the use of the Balanced Scorecard approach with corrective action plans (/Soe-99/ p. 20, et seq.).

An example on supplier performance measurement from a case study is presented by Ogden and McCarter (/Ogd-04/). The considered company attained higher value by evaluating the performance in the areas product & technology, service and support, quality, delivery & lead-time and the total cost performance: When there are gaps the supplier has to improve to meet the requirements, leading to other suppliers' motivation to improve also. The considered company gives incentives (awards) to its supplier's. The resulting benefits are long term commitment, the close relationship decreases risks (which are shared by both companies), and the top management is involved in quarterly performance reviews. Also Min (/Min-98/) presents a best practice in which it was recognized that a control program is essential for continuous improvement. Measuring performance, creation of improvement targets with the suppliers, and the facilitation of the supplier's understanding were understood as the drivers to achieve the goal.

2.3.3 Supplier Management

Many companies have divisions, which are responsible for supplier management and that are rather involved in production processes, negotiations and relationship management than being directly involved into the operative tasks of the procurement. Hartmann (/Har-04/ p. 100, et seq.) describes the risks and chances to consider in supplier management. Besides of the size of the company, its policy and strategy, there are some fundamental circumstances, which play an essential role in supplier management:

- A high qualification of the participating employees, regarding their competency in technology, methodology, leading and organization, is required (as in the sales).

- Negotiations with the suppliers, which are considered to be partners, have to be executed with changing buyer's employees. Decisions have to be found in a team.

- The procurement employees need to know about the supplier's strategy, since economic circumstances (e.g. low orders) may drive his decisions. Therefore supplier controlling and site visits are inevitable.

- The best opportunity for a successful supplier management is the win-win situation. Both parties have to see the benefits of a contract and a prosperous future development. For both sides there is supposed be the strong desire for a long term partnership.

- A weaker market position bares risks for the weaker partner. Since the sourcing volume is small he can't count with a real partnership from the other side.

- Insufficient controlling bears the risk that economic problems are not recognized and cannot be avoided in time. Therefore a preventive risk management is necessary.

As the major chances for a successful partnership Hartmann understands the standardization, simultaneous engineering, the learning curve effect to decrease prices, and the optimization of the entire supply chain. Further, Hartmann states that supporting activities (e.g. workshops) at the supplier's site may be required in order to attain the desired partnership. However, this needs funding and capacities. Eventually, the basis for a long term partnership between employees and organizations are trust and open communication.

2.3.4 Supplier Controlling

According to Hartmann (/Har-04/ p. 93, et seq.), the supplier controlling can be divided into strategic and operative supplier controlling. The operative controlling includes the assessment/the measurement, which leads to certain action. The most important tasks of the operative supplier controlling are the monitoring of the supply performance, the early recognition of changes of the performance, and the recognition and understanding of deficits. So, it enables supplier improvement activities and forms the information basis for the strategic controlling. The strategic controlling in contrast, deals with the realization of strategies, as far as they have impact on the measures within the operative controlling. However, the strategic controlling is more qualitative in nature: it presents the strengths and weaknesses, the risks and chances.

Although the strategic controlling regularly does not have a short term impact on the buyer supplier relationship, it influences it on the mid and long term. In contrast to the past, when only the price, quality and reliability were considered, the strategic controlling has to emphasize the dynamics of orders and the flexibility regarding changing circumstances, lean management of procurement, logistics and modern IT-systems. The competitiveness of a company, however, can be increased only by the implementation of future-oriented methods and concepts. Still conservative indicators are justifiable and have to be included, but an operative-strategic supplier management concept requires according to Hartmann an analysis of the (operative) measures, resulting in mutually decided strategic objectives, which have mid or long term effect (/Har-04/ p. 98, et seq.).

2.3.5 Supplier's Capabilities

The capabilities of a supplier are defined in different ways. In this research they are defined as the "ability to fulfill the (buyer's) requirements". They can be broken down in sub-capabilities making it possible to differentiate between different business functions and business processes, which form the basis for the resulting capabilities.

In the beginning of a buyer supplier relationship, supplier's capabilities are often not meeting the performance- or even the minimum requirements of the buying organization. Most capabilities are dependent on the supplier structure, which is being assessed within the supplier audit, which is one of the preliminary actions of improvement conducted by a cross-functional, risk-assessment team [*equivalent to audit-team*]. Some typically assessed criteria consider the Quality-, Cost-reduction-, technical-, project management-, cycle time- , and other (cap-) abilities (cp. /Han-99/ p. 31).

In an example given by Handfield, a company describes its improvement activities as "fixing things". The following figure (Figure 2.3) shows the process of increasing maturity of the company's new suppliers. Supplier Improvement A ("S-Dev (A)") is the process of fostering mutual understanding of the necessary capabilities in order to stay business partners. The processes from supplier Improvement B ("S-Dev (B)") on have the aim to integrate the supplier, in order to increase efficiency and cooperation. It can be said that this activities are mostly reactive in nature (/Han-99/ p. 33).

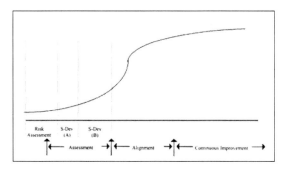

Figure 2.3 Supplier Maturity Curve (/Han-99/ p. 32)

2.4 Global sourcing

When an IC company decides to commence global sourcing, it has the aim to penetrate the market or to leverage the specific advantages of the foreign country's resources to stay competitive. In this work, latter motivation is considered to be the driver of China activities. This means, that the attainment of products at competitive costs is the goal to achieve.

According to Appelfeller (/App-05/ p. 64, et seq.) the chances of global sourcing can be among others the following two. First, the advantage of saving costs by leveraging the lower prices in the foreign country to increase the company's competitiveness, by sourcing from there or building a local production site. Or second, the penetration of new supply markets and future sales markets. Naturally, global sourcing takes in risks as well. Delivery and quality performance may be lacking due to different quality mentality. The reliability, flexibility and innovation may be poor and difficult to assure. The total cost of ownership may not be considered. The scheduling and transportation issues can represent drawbacks due to the big distance and the high capital lockup. Other environmental risks, which are not influence able, for example politics and catastrophes may occur.

2.4.1 Low-cost sources in global procurement

Buyers, who allocate their supply chain to other countries to leverage the advantages of e.g. lower labor costs, have to consider that the establishment of a localized supply base in another country with a full extent to support local production and sales is difficult (/Han-02/). A reason for this process being critical is that companies have to source a significant part of their production locally, since governments are increasingly pushing Local Content laws. The relationships with the new suppliers are hardly the same as in the home market. However, in some cases [e.g. China], local supplier's production capabilities may be too low to meet the buyer's requirements, like production technology, engineering and design abilities, information systems, quality and delivery reliability (/Han-02/).

As a success factor companies recognize supplier improvement (e.g. /Dun-04/; /Han-00/; /Har-97/ and others). Resources can be invested into a team of specialists that assesses suppliers and improves their capabilities to meet the requirements in a short period. An approach, which tells the supplier how to increase his level of capabilities (with a report on the deficits and suggestions how to fix them) saves the supplier burden (/Han-99/ p. 33). Handfield (/Han-02/ p. 113) states that "leading organizations do not simply tell the supplier to improve, but are increasingly adopting a hands-on approach to improvement, which often involves working directly with the supplier to identify and resolve problems".

2.4.2 Considerations for Sourcing in China

In this work's case the buyer follows a strategy, which can be referred to as "global integration"(/Kau-05/): Kaufmann describes it as a strategy that includes high value-adding in foreign countries and a high internal transfer of goods and services. With this strategy, a company connects different business processes allocated to countries, where the local advantages are used to leverage the competitiveness. The major goal of this strategy is to use these advantages of resources and local efficiencies the best. So, the example of sourcing in China to use the leverage of low labor cost is applicable. However, it has to be considered, that often the resulting risk can be critical and reduce the savings drastically.

Kaufmann (/Kau-05/ p. 165) states that the number of capable suppliers is growing steadily, so the sourcing in China is increasingly possible. Especially mid and long term strategies have prospect for success. However, Kaufmann explains that challenges like the unavailability of expensive production technology, the problem for Chinese suppliers to maintain good supplier buyer relationships, and the high volatility of quality (despite of the reachable quality level) are still a big drawback in the Chinese market. However, as part of a mid and long term strategy, investments in certain areas can facilitate the success in the Chinese market. Kaufmann and Salmi (/Kau-05/ p. 169; /Sal-05/) identify following as major drivers for success:

(1) The procurement has to be integrated strongly into the business processes, as it has a high importance in the Chinese market (due to the mentioned difficulties).

(2) Performance has to be steadily measured and quality controlled.

(3) The suppliers are major factors for the competitiveness achieved in China. So, supplier development and improvement (technical, managerial and also financial support) are to be executed: development of a reliable supply base, investments into quality improvement and the education of the procurement staff are of fundamental importance for the procurement.

(4) Education and training of the procurement professionals to gain the knowledge and skills required for the Chinese market.

(5) Consideration of the cultural issues (from here cp. /Sal-05/).

(6) Product specifications have to be understood clearly.

(7) Foster trust to support the discussion of problems ("losing the face issue"), local presence is required.

(8) Building of the relationship network (Guanxi[1]; further comments on this are given in chapter 2.4.6).

(9) Another possibility to avoid problems is the "supplier-following-OEM approach", when suppliers from the home market follow to China (/Kau-05/ p. 169). [*author's comment: in this case latter ones would be considered as buyers*]

---

[1] Guanxi is a network of personal relations in the Chinese culture; it represent an important and powerful part of private and business relationships – it has to be built up, fostered and applied correctly in order to gain benefits from it (cp. /Hu-05/; /Sat-05/)

2.4.3 Procurement Activities in China

Not only in China the supplier relationship management and improvement are significant tasks of the procurement. However, in China this is extraordinarily important, since the supplier's capabilities are often lacking to meet the buyer's requirements.

Hence, in China the practices from operational up to the strategic procurement activities have to be applied (see Figure 2.4). Special emphasis has to be given to the quality assurance and, since it is a big problem, to the delivery reliability (cp. chapter 2.4.4). The "coordinated/leveraged" activities have to focus the supplier relations in China, since the Guanxi is recommended to be considered as cultural characteristic. The proper application of latter one can be powerful to decrease risks and manage present problems. In contrast, not considering it may take in disadvantages (cp. /Sat-05/; /Hu-05/). Also the supplier certification and the supplier performance measurement are required in China, since they represent opportunities to decrease risk (for the business generally, and also for the success of supply). The strategic part of the presented activities includes many activities, which are essential if sourcing in the Chinese market (compare interview results in chapter 4). So, e.g. the supplier improvement programs, as well as the internal training programs can help the buyer's employees to learn the different issues in China and how to approach Chinese suppliers. The performance measurement builds the basis for the improvement as well as the planning and strategic decision making.

	Activities	Organization implication
Strategic	- Direction and policy setting - Human resource coordination - Achieve global transparency of sorts and suppliers and give periodic feedback - Performance management - Supply strategy and planning - Supplier development programs - Internal training programs - Coordinate all important procurement activities	- Transparency in policies, roles, activities, contracts in place - Common understanding - Highly skilled personnel - Lean staff
Coordinate/Leveraged	- Commodity supply strategy - Supplier certification - Supplier relations - Sourcing activities - Supplier performance measurement - Contract negotiations	- Clear mix of centralized and decentralized - Key commodities - High spend items - Use of purchasing councils to coordinate
Operational	- Purchase order processing - Expediting - Quality assurance and inspection - Invoice processing/payment - Material control and inventory	- Decentralized and automated

Figure 2.4 Procurement activities performed at different levels (/Soe-99/)

Supplier Development and Improvement in China

The following is based on the findings from the interviews conducted in the scope of this work, discussed in chapter 4.

Supplier development and improvement is, besides of strategic cooperation, material group sourcing and parallel negotiations, one of the most important methods of procurement in

China. It includes principally the same steps as in Industrialized Countries, but the single proceedings have to be rethought. Already the identification of the product to source and the supplier finding have to focus on the possible pitfalls and risks. The following supplier- and risk assessment has a high relevancy, as it decides over further cooperation: regularly, the same proceedings like in ICs are used, but subjective factors have a much higher relevancy in most companies. After identifying the critical elements of the supplier's business, an improvement plan has to be set up and monitored during the following relationship.

Improvement talks and planning with the suppliers are common practice in ICs. Since companies regularly use company-wide concepts, the supplier improvement in China has mostly the same structure. However, supplier improvement in China has rather fundamental problems to cover than an optimization of suppliers in IC's. A minimum level of capabilities has to be attained in order to mitigate the risk of non-delivery or unsatisfying parts. Many risks threatening a successful supply of required parts make a holistic improvement important in China. Undertaking actions to decrease risks and to enhance the major required processes helps to mitigate the probability that the costs eventually exceed the expected savings due to an unexpected problem.

When developing a supplier in China, buyers aim for following goals to build up a successful relationship (supposing striving for savings for bought-in parts):

- Maintain supply quality and reliability and achieve savings at the same time. The calculation of savings has to include all additionally caused costs to obtain the required bought-in-part and the financially expressed risk.

- Commit the supplier to the relationship. He has to know and understand the buyer's requirements and facilitate the fulfillment of it. For the supplier this means learning and a partnership-oriented strategy.

- Improve the supplier's capabilities and the mutual relationship to decrease response time, in order to increase efficiency and to develop a competitive buyer supplier relationship with both companies profiting from these improvements.

These goals are stretching - it is unlikely that a supplier matching these goals from the beginning can be found, nevertheless, they can be used as orientation. Deeper considerations on supplier development and improvement with regard on China are done within the desktop research in chapter 3.1 and within the suggested approach in chapter 6.

2.4.4 Differences between markets

In the scope of this work a survey and interviews were conducted with companies located in Germany and China regarding their China (sourcing) activity. The following findings are based on latter ones (if no other reference is given).

In order to stay globally competitive, already most of Industrialized-Country (IC) companies source products or services from Low-Cost-Countries (LCC). Especially sourcing from China is increasingly important (see following graph Figure 2.1). The sourced products are becoming more advanced in technology in the next years. IC companies stated that they expect a procurement-ratio of about 10% for each A and B parts by 2010 in China (today this ratio is near to zero).

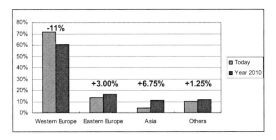

Figure 2.5 Increase of average sourcing quota in the world by 2010

For the considered industry (mechanical engineering investment goods) the main reasons for shifting are the entry of a new sales market in first place, since China is developing very fast, including a growing competition for IC companies. As a further important reason the cost savings of procured goods are mentioned.

Often a great part of the production costs can be determined by bought-in part costs. Sourcing from China means using the leverage of low labor cost, and has the intention to facilitate the global competitiveness. IC Companies expect a cost saving potential between 20 % and 60 %. In the following, it is assumed that the buyers' main intention is to achieve savings with their LCC-procurement-activity.

2.4.5 China specific issues

There are diverse problems, which make sourcing in China risky and the supplier improvement in China necessary. These problems are not restricted to insufficient efficiency. They are of elementary nature instead. The most common problems occurring whilst developing a supplier in China are shown in the following graph. Quality and delivery reliability problems occur frequently, both representing serious issues and big risk-factors. As shown, latter ones are of a much higher relevancy than the following issues emerging. Most IC-companies have Chinese employees, who help to lower the communication and understanding barrier regarding the specifications – in contrast, the comprehension of a certain company culture towards customers and products represents a bigger issue. Strategy and market situation determine the cooperation willingness. Despite of the mentioned problems with certain suppliers, the overall willingness is considered to be good. Critical risks endangering the benefits of the China sourcing activity, rank together with an unexpected rise of price last, but are evidently present as well.

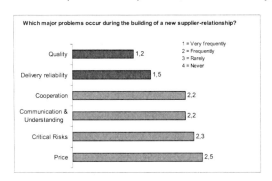

Figure 2.6 Graph showing the major problems occurring

Some companies decrease the major risks by parallel sourcing (one part from at least two suppliers) so that switching is possible in the case of instable quality and delivery. Other companies have even "backup" from their home organization in the ICs, to substitute parts. Both solutions are not efficient and satisfying. A holistic supplier development and improvement in contrast, tries to assure that the requirements are reliably met by one (all) supplier(s) in China.

Risks and Chances

In the times of demand for increased flexibility and varieties, short reaction times and integrated approaches the development of a new supply base in a distance of thousands of miles seems to be highly challenging, if not unreasonable. In contrast, from the viewpoint of possible savings (which can be passed on to the customer), strategic market penetration and positioning, the chances seem to be worth the risks. But, latter ones need to be monitored and decreased, because they take in the potential to reduce the expected savings and benefits.

The creation of a new supply base always includes at least one other company: the Chinese supplier. Many procurement managers (participants of the survey described in chapter 4) feel that China has an uncountable amount of suppliers, but only a small number of them are capable to reliably supply the required products (this fact is shown in Illustration 2.4). In fact, latter ones are in particular cases even more expensive than their IC competitors. These are regularly not taken into account, since it is aspired to achieve savings. Thus, the buyers often have to compromise – the resulting relationship with the Chinese "low-cost-supplier" has normally a big potential for improvement.

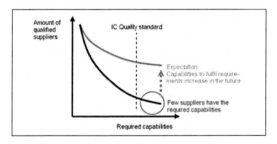

Illustration 2.7: Few suppliers seem capable of fulfilling requirements

High requirements vs. lacking capabilities

Customers ordering specialized machines or whole solutions from the considered industry have high demands in quality and delivery reliability. These demands are passed on to the suppliers, as bought-in parts represent a significant part of the finalized product. Accordingly, the buyer (the OEM) has to minimize the risk of inadequate quality and delivery. The price ranks after these first requirements, but has to be lower than the IC price after considering all costs emerging through the sourcing in China (supplier development, supplier management, transportation etc.). These requirements face the supplier's capabilities, which are concluded by his business-structure including all product-related business-functions. Further, the understanding of and commitment to quality and the differing strategy, although difficult to measure, play a big role as they are fundamental elements of co-operational competence.

Most critical risks occurring

The risks in China differ broadly from the risks occurring on the home market of the IC companies. The table below (Figure 2.8) shows the critical risks specified by companies involved in procurement in China. As the most critical risks were mentioned: the infringement of patent and the know-how transfer to competitors; the attainment of low quality due to insufficient quality control at the supplier's site (can often be related to sub-suppliers); and, based on communication issues and cultural differences, the occurring communication problems leading to misunderstandings. As mentioned, many of these risks can be decreased strongly by supplier improvement activities. Even more, if the supplier improvement is integrated in a well executed supplier development process. However, both supplier development and improvement underlie environmental and business related conditions, which influence the effect and success of the buyer's intentions.

Figure 2.8 Emerging critical risks during procurement in China

2.4.6 Differences in aims and company culture in ICs and China

The increased sourcing due to the concentration on core competencies makes the buyer dependent on relying on his suppliers. By the means of market power (sourcing volume, brand and image), the buyer has the possibility to push suppliers to undertake changes. First, this serves mainly the buyer, who wants to know his requirements fulfilled. However, the supplier benefits eventually from increased order-volumes and higher business efficiency. The supplier has also direct impact on the possibilities of the supplier improvement process, as he is the 2nd link. Consequently, suppliers who want to expand their sales to overseas companies are motivated to support a partnership with an IC buyer, because it contributes to the important reputation (findings from interviews). In contrast, if a supplier is mostly independent by having "enough orders" or a big market power (/Har-04/), the interest might be lower.

As one of the major differences in China, the cultural one has to be mentioned. So for example the building of personal relationships (Guanxi), plays a big role not only in personal life but in business also (cp. also /Hu-05/; /Sat-05/). According to Salmi (/Sal-05/) the Guanxi can compensate the lacking of a developed legal framework and support negotiations. As part of the culture, "losing the face" (/Kro-98/; /Sal-05/) is an issue that often can lead to misunderstandings due to another meaning of "yes" or "no". This is also an issue within the Chinese companies, when the employees don't give feedback on a problem to save the own supervisor's face towards the senior. Further, the business culture and the strategies differ strongly. The market is fast changing and the business management is often short term profit oriented, so that commitment to a buyer, who sources only low volume, is often unprivileged compared to an incoming high volume order (/Har-04/). In addition, the interviews found that the supplier often don't supply directly the quality level they are capable of, but try it with lower level first. This is an issue especially in the beginning of an IC company's China sourcing activities.

However, on the other side there are positive aspects of the Chinese business culture, which can facilitate the planed activities as long as taken advantage of them in the right way. So, e.g. the personal involvement can be mentioned: if properly applying the principle of Guanxi, inter-organizational business processes, also beyond its borders can be supported enormously. Further, the problem solving skills of Chinese employees are considered to be high and creative, which with the correct approach may be motivated to change shortcomings. The open minded business management allows site visits with low barriers, which is rather unusual in Industrialized Countries. The short term profit orientation is confronted by the willingness to improvement (according Wilson (/Wil-95/ p. 34) high among production line workers) and long term cooperation (both confirmed in the interviews). Also by Salmi (/Sal-05/), the long term orientation and the aim "win-win situation" are identified as characteristics to consider in the Chinese business culture.

2.5 The Balanced Scorecard

2.5.1 General framework

The Balanced Scorecard (BSC) was introduced by Kaplan and Norton in the year 1996, presenting a concept, which allows the translation of an "organization's mission and strategy into a comprehensive set of performance measures that provides the framework for a strategic measurement and management system" (/BSC-06/).

It is meant to be a strategic management system that includes and "balances", in contrast to other performance measurement approaches, not only the financial perspective, but also the customer perspective, the internal processes and the learning and growth perspective of a business. These perspectives are the necessary businesses-elements that drive success. In addition, one of the major advantages of this approach is that it includes not only past figures, but also the current ones (showing the current situation). Further, it contains intangible assets, which represent the company's intangible capital that enables the value to be added: human, information and organization capital and the growth of it (/Kap-04/ p.2).

Ruggiero states that the Balanced Scorecard as performance measurement scheme is able to (cp. /Rug-06/):

- Express the strategic vision of a firm
- Connect strategic goals to suitable performance indicators
- Communicate objectives and measures to the whole organization
- Plan, program and suggest strategies and goals to achieve long term results
- Develop and improve the strategic feed-back process.

The Balanced Scorecard is a tool to measure the progress of the company towards its strategic objectives. It publishes the performance targets set, lists the strategic initiatives aligned to its targets, and measures the success against the objectives (/Cre-05/p. 6). The following Figure 2.9 shows a template BSC.

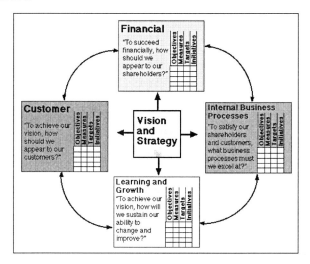

Figure 2.9 A template Balanced Scorecard (cp. /Arv-98/)

Although the Balanced Scorecard is meant to be a strategic management tool, companies discovered its advantages for performance measurement and monitoring. Handfield (/Han-02/ p. 69) writes that a good performance measurement system is "actionable", so that it enables managers not only to identify, but also to solve the given problems. He presents the Balanced Scorecard as a suitable approach for the supply chain performance measurement. With its strategy, objectives and measures, it can be taken from the management level down to the team level, where, within each perspective, objectives and strategies can be fixed according to the superior strategies and objectives.

However, many other authors, who see the Balanced Scorecard as a usable method in Supply Chain management, felt that the original BSC has to be adapted in terms of its perspectives or their orientation. Many companies change the shape of the BSCs, to fit them into their companies leading strategies and objectives (further details in chapter 3.2).

2.5.2 Strategy maps

"Strategy maps" are an "extension" of the Balanced Scorecard: Kaplan and Norton (/Kap-04/) introduce them as tool to show the linkages between the intangible and tangible assets, respectively between the strategic objectives, in cause-and-effect relationships.

The strategy map and the Balanced Scorecard include the same perspectives. The BSC is aligning all objectives to measures (target/status) and initiatives. With this, it is possible to measure improvement and manage the action to achieve a certain target. For this "steering", the strategy map was found to be a strongly supportive tool, to articulate and manage strategy and to translate it to the operational level (Figure 2.10). It ensures that the strategic objectives found are consistent and can be aligned internally, so that there is no objective working not supportive or even against another one.

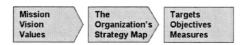

Figure 2.10 From Vision to Strategy Map to Balanced Scorecard

In the first instance, there has to be defined a well recognizable and by all participating members understandable and motivating strategy. Creelman and Makhijani (/Cre-05/ p. 135) write that it represents a vision, which is inspirational and ideally includes the major activities of the business. Since it shows what the BSC's strategic objectives have to aim for, it also posses the same business perspectives (regularly four) as the BSC. The strategy map is built in the following sequence (/Kap-04/): The financial perspective is the main goal, since it represents the value for the shareholders. There are two strategic objectives in the financial perspective. It is the growth and the productivity, between which a "balance" has to be found: the balance between long-term growth by investing into the entity, and short-term productivity increase by cutting costs. Latter one can also be achieved by short term improvements. The customer perspective represents the buyer requirements and the value demanded. The customer perspective drives the objectives in the financial perspective. Therefore, the products and/ or service value has to be as high as possible for the customer (e.g. lowest total cost of ownership, superior products and services etc.). The internal perspective includes the business processes, which are responsible for creating the value for the customer. They have to be improved and attain a high level, in order to create higher value at lower cost. The fourth perspective is the learning and growth perspective, which includes the intangible assets of the company: its information system, its organizational capital, and as the most important the employees, who run the business, the "human capital".

The strategy map has advantages, which are described briefly in the following (cp. /Kap-04/ p.2):

- Financially it supports the decision making in terms of investment. It shows which strategy has to be prioritized financially, to support the long-term growth or boost the short-term results.

- Enables the comparison of a company with the competitors, and thus, helps to articulate an individual strategy that increases the value for the customer

- Supports the balancing of resources for the internal processes in order to attain benefits constantly

- (…)

Kaplan and Norton write (/Kap-04/ p.3) "in summary, the strategy map template, customized to the organization's particular strategy, describes how intangible assets drive performance enhancements to the organization's internal processes that have the maximum leverage for delivering value to customers, shareholders and communities."

2.5.3 Key Performance Indicators / Measures

The performance indicators of the Balanced Scorecard differ from the widely used ones (in Supply Chain Management). The difference is caused by the strategic and forward looking orientation of the BSC. Nowadays, companies change their thinking on this topic. Whereat conservative performance indicators like quality, delivery and price keep being highly important, today the focus is laid also on indicators on the health of relationships, on indicators, which are more forward looking (cp. /Har-04/ p. 98, et seq.).

The Balanced Scorecard is not a pure measurement system, it is meant to comprise the strategic objectives, related measures, targets and initiatives that support the strategy map's aims. The amount of strategic objectives requires reduction to the "critical few ones". The same limitation counts for the strategic measures. Strategic measures have the aim of assessing progress towards the objective. This measurement is based on "leading and lagging" measures. Each of them has to be clearly defined and has to have an owner aligned. The given targets need to be achievable although stretching and time-bound in order to foster motivation. The strategic initiatives are the actions to undertake to reduce the distance of actual-state to target (cp. /Cre-05/ p. 155, et seqq.). The lagging measures represent already past events (e.g. delayed delivery, rework rate for the last order) and thus, describe past performance, but are not able to tell about the development in the future. In contrast, leading measures are forward looking: They are measures, which show what currently is happening and will have impact on future performance. A measure can also be both leading and lagging, since certain past indicators enable a deduction on the future development (e.g. customer satisfaction, as it has impact on future sales/turnover/image) (cp. /Cre-05/ p. 155, et seq.).

Since definitions of measures may be different from organization to organization, from IC buyer to Chinese supplier, the measures need to be clearly defined and understood, especially by the measures' owners, who are responsible for the measuring. Often the stretching targets wouldn't be reached in time. This can facilitate to rethink the initiative and so, to improve the actions. Eventually, these initiatives are the executed solutions promising the increase of capabilities. Naturally, these initiatives have to be assessed upon their importance, impact, and their effort needed (cp. /Cre-05/ p. 160, et seq.).

3 State of the Art in Research

Companies that aim for leveraging the low cost sourcing potential of China in order to stay competitive, regularly face problems and barriers. One of the main barriers is represented by the suppliers, which often seem not to be capable of supplying the requested product. The supplier development and improvement is an approach that emerged in the 1990s. Its origin lies in the buyer's concentration on core competencies and his rising dependency on the suppliers. The aim is to decrease risk and enhance efficiency (/Han-99/; /Soe-99/).

Therefore, desktop research provides the known concepts of supplier development and improvement, presenting the known barriers and benefits. Further, literature review shows that the approach of the Balanced Scorecard is suitable to tackle this issue, since it can combine the tangible and intangible assets of a relationship and support the short term decision making based on a strategic orientation. Especially in an intercultural and interorganizational relationship, not only the production processes are responsible for a successful supply. This is particularly not the case for the development of a prosperous partnership-oriented relationship that allows steady improvement. So, after the desktop research, the findings from the conducted industry survey are presented to identify the main problems IC Companies are faced with, when penetrating the Chinese supply market. Furthermore, the drivers of success and the practical approaches are recognized, in order to design a method that supports the improvement of the given relationship lastingly.

3.1 Supplier Development and Improvement

3.1.1 Supplier Development

3.1.1.1 The supplier development process (/Dun-04/)

Dunn and Young describe the supplier development as a proceeding, which has the objective to eventually align the supplier's capabilities with the buyer's expectations. Already the preliminary steps are described to be part of the supplier development process (Phase 1), and are required in order to reach the final objective. The found structure of supplier development is shown in the following figure (Figure 3.1) (the "development activities" mean "supplier improvement activities" according this work's definition).

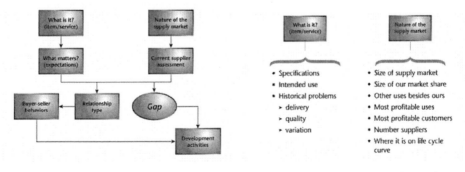

Figure 3.1 Supplier development process (/Dun-04/)   Figure 3.2 Phase 1: Constraints (/Dun-04/)

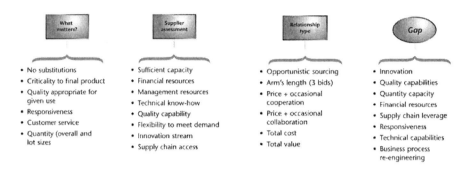

Figure 3.3 Phase 2: Specifications and Requirements (/Dun-04/)

Figure 3.4 Phase 3: The relationship and the needs (/Dun-04/)

In the first phase (Figure 3.2), the constraints based on the item to source have to be deduced and translated to the buyer's expectations. Upon these expectations, the supply market can be analyzed and assessed upon suitability for the buyer. The second phase (Figure 3.3) has to identify the buyer's desired values: based on the product specifications, experiences and expectations, they lead to the requirements towards the supplier. The supplier has to be assessed regarding processes and capabilities. An additional part of this step is the creation of the mutual understanding of the system of conduct to solve conflicts of interest. It is one of the buyer's requirements, which the supplier has to understand and adhere to satisfy the buyer. In the third phase (Figure 3.3) the gaps between the buyer's requirements and the supplier's capabilities have to be found. One of the main possible difficulties is the measurement and the communication of these findings. Further, the discussion of strategic partnership orientation is crucial, if both companies want to benefit from the relationship. The price of the undertaking may be high, but the long term cost is assuredly low.

Following factors are identified as drivers of success (including, but not limited to):

- the clear assignment of representatives at all key levels, which create a single communication line
- an accurate measurement of savings to determine the profit potential
- the establishment of communication loops, with individuals as key representatives for all implementation issues
- both organizations have to be able to use the same criteria for easy measurement of success or failure
- and, the paradigm has to change from a "us against them" to a "we".

Conclusion

Dunn and Young describe the supplier development from the beginning up to the improvement of capabilities in order to attain a partnership oriented relationship. However, this approach does not describe further steps of the improvement activities, or makes a differentiation of the supplier improvement process in terms of organization, type or involvement. Further the question remains, whether the development process in another country would differ from the suggested one by Dunn and Young. This gives room for further research. But still, drivers of success of the supplier improvement process are described and can be extracted.

3.1.1.2 Pitfalls in Supplier Development (/Han-00/)

Another approach by Handfield aims to identify the critical issues in supplier development. Handfield states that most companies' practices in supplier development can be approached by a seven-step process. The identified steps are according Handfield (/Han-00/ p. 40) the following ones.

> "Step 1: Identify Critical Commodities
>
> Step 2: Identify Critical Suppliers
>
> Step 3: Form a Cross-Functional Team
>
> Step 4: Meet with Supplier Top Management
>
> Step 5: Identify Key Projects
>
> Step 6: Define Details of Agreement
>
> Step 7: Monitor Status and Modify Strategies"

According to Handfield most of the companies considered in the related research were satisfied with their development success, since total cost, quality, delivery performance and other supplier's characteristics were enhanced. But on the other side, there are the companies, which didn't attain the expected outcomes due to problems (from supplier's side, buyer's side or problems occurring between both companies). Most of the considered companies have problems to apply the steps form the fifth step on. Out of these issues, some are mentioned to have major root causes: problems emerge during meetings between buyer and supplier management teams, when defining key projects, determining agreement terms or measures for success and when monitoring project status and subsequently modifying strategies.

Handfield suggest the buyer's team to delineate potential rewards already in early meetings with the supplier's management, in order to foster its commitment to cooperation. Handfield concludes that in order to attain success in supplier development, the buyer has to be committed and "infect" the supplier with this commitment. Early understanding for both sides and the discussion of cost sharing is the basis. Afterwards, measures and timelines give the foundation for the record and the joint problem solving. He stresses that relationship management and strategic emphasis are critical to success, as unsupportive managers are often a reason for failure.

From the case studies presented (/Han-00/ p. 41 et seqq.), approaches to manage suppliers are shown. In the case of occurring communication and understanding problems, it was found that stronger involvement and personal discussions are necessary for the supplier's employees' business culture to be aligned to the buyer's expectations. Further, these expectations are fixed in a so called Expectation Road Map to encourage the buyer/supplier alignment by showing the short, medium and long term objectives.

Conclusion

This research includes the main steps of the supplier development process. Critical factors for success are shown, and suggestions to avoid issues are made. However, regarding the issues in

China, for example the suggestion, to consolidate fewer suppliers to illustrate the value of supplier development, is highly questionable, since it increases the supply risk eminently. The presented approach is rather IC companies oriented (than global or China specific), so the steps may lack of consideration of global occurring issues. Nevertheless, the commonly emerging issues with key projects, terms, measures, and monitoring may occur in any situation between e.g. buyer and supplier. Therefore, the buyer supplier relationship has to be emphasized as well. The suggestion to create a so called Expectation Road Map may have positive influence on a "Chinese Supplier - IC Buyer Relationship" as well, but there are no details given on its shape and its characteristics.

3.1.2 Supplier Development in China

A recent approach by Fleischer (/Fle-06/) shows the required steps to undertake in order to develop a new supplier in China. It partially includes steps of supplier development presented in the chapters before, but is extended, since it regards the China specific characteristics.

When intending to show the main steps to accomplish when developing a new Chinese supplier, milestones and main processes have to be appointed and an integrative and extensive model is required. The purpose is to achieve a process model which may be used as guideline, from the decision to China-sourcing on to after-sales-service cooperation in the end. Therefore, the general supplier development approaches need to get enlarged with further steps: First, the appropriate product to source has to be chosen. The next step consists in identifying the proper supplier. The process of sourcing from China is completed by the integration of a supplier assessment process. Summarizing, a supplier development process model for low-cost countries is proposed that consists of seven stages (/Fle-06/) (see Figure 3.5).

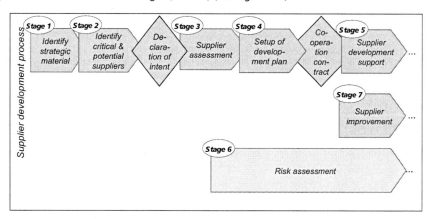

Figure 3.5 Supplier development process (/Fle-06/)

Stages 1-3 are to identify a supplier, which has to be capable to fulfill the future requirements on the supply. Since the sourcing from China includes other risks and problems than the sourcing in the home market, the stages to consider have to be adapted. These first stages are described in the following paragraphs (further information in (/Wag-06/)).

3.1.2.1 Stage 1: Selection of relevant supplied parts

The decision of sourcing from a low-cost country may be made on account of a well suited commodity or the choice is based on the organization's strategy. The latter case requires the finding of a proper commodity, which ideally has a big potential of saving costs and at the same time does take in as less risks as possible. Accordingly, stage 1 ("identify strategic material") is influenced significantly by the three factors purchasing volume (1), complexity of the sourced commodity (2) and complexity of technology of manufacturing this commodity (3). These factors contain a main influence on the savings that can be achieved in the end. Especially the third point "technology" has to be recognized due to the danger of violation of patents. In case of plagiarism the achieved savings might get diminished dramatically. In addition, product related characteristics such as logistics, quality attainment, cost structure, a need for R&D, cooperation as well as after-sales and environmental issues play an elementary role in choosing the proper commodity. Since the commodity to deliver is one of the main drivers for both risk and costs, an integrative view of the supplier development process is essential (/Fle-06/).

3.1.2.2 Stage 2: Selection of relevant suppliers & Declaration of intent

In stage 2 ("Identify critical & potential suppliers"), an appropriate supplier has to be found in the country of preference. This procedure is similar to the commodity properties mainly influenced by the strategy and the risk management of the buying organization. Having identified an appropriate supplier a meeting between the supplier top management and the buying organization's cross-functional team has to be realized. A paperwork that may be called "declaration of intent" ratifies the required steps of action, both for the supplier and the buying organization and represents the start of the future collaboration (/Fle-06/).

Wagner (/Wag-06/) presents the primary (buyer actively involved into investigation) and secondary information sources (external companies' data is used).

Primary information sources	Secondary information sources
•Trade shows •Supplier self-disclosure •Meetings/Experience exchange •Market research institutes •Personal contacts •Company/ plant visit •Offers •Samples •Internal sources	•Chamber of commerce and industry (IHK) •Governmental institute for information of foreign affairs (BfAi) •Non-governmental organizations •Publications/ statistical analyses of governmental institute for statistics •Foundations (e.g. International Federation of Purchasing and Material Management (IFPMM) •Databases •Internet (homepages, virtual market places,...) •Newspapers/ magazines (general/ special) •References •Company lists •Stock exchange/ market reports •Publications of suppliers

Figure 3.6 Information sources for supplier identification (/Wag-06/)

Further Wagner (/Wag-06/) presents an overview over product dependent supplier qualification and the proceeding to advance to the step of "declaration of intent". The declaration of intent is a paperwork, which has to secure both companies' discretion in order to avoid information misuse. After completing these preliminary steps successfully, the supplier of choice is being assessed in order to identify in deep information on the supplier's capabilities and deficiencies.

3.1.2.3 Stage 3: Supplier assessment to determine status quo

At this point the cooperation can start with the supplier assessment. Also the main part of supplier development begins, since the assessment is the decision-point for future collaboration and also the supplier improvement. In order to find the supplier's critical characteristics, we recommend the accomplishment of a joint assessment of the supplying organization at first. Supplier risk assessment is an important task of the supplier development team: The cross-functional team completes a questionnaire after having spent some days at the supplier's site, ascertaining the personnel's knowledge and evaluating their processes. At the end of the visit, the supplier receives the results of the audit, and follow-up visits are scheduled as necessary (/Fle-06/).

The Audit is suggested as one major part for the assessment of the supplier. It is a systematic and independent investigation, which strives for a detailed overview over the supplier's business processes, or in other words, the present and lacking capabilities. After the evaluation, a report with a list of improvement suggestions is given to the supplier. This report is an important document for the future improvement activities, since it shows the connections between recommended changes and the causes of problems identified in the audit. The deficits are described by certain percentages of fulfillment and need improvement in order of relevancy. Because of the different cultures, relationship management plays an essential role during these joint activities; also each company needs an individual consideration (/Wag-06/).

Wagner further presents a complete supplier assessment tool in order to uncover the supplier's performance level and the supplier's potential with regard to the main supply targets. The achievement of latter ones depends on the key capabilities ("cost and service", "quality", "logistics", "technology", "cooperation willingness" and "financial situation"). Therefore, the key capabilities form the basis for the measurement system. Different assessment methods are combined to the tool. A criteria set is presented, which gives an overview of the aspects included in the assessment tool (/Wag-06/). The basic structure can be approached by the following table (Figure 3.7).

	L1 – key competences	%	L2 – Improvement Components	%	L3 – Criteria	%
Total Score = max 100 points	Cost & Service	xx	1.1. Pricing aspects	xx	1.1.1. Transparent cost structure	xx
			1.2. Purchasing conditions	xx	1.1.2. Price fixing	xx
			1.3. ...	xx	1.1.3. Prices for spares	xx
					1.1.4.	
	Quality	xx	...	xx	...	xx
	Logistics	xx	...	xx	...	xx
	Cooperation	xx	...	xx	...	xx
		xx		xx	...	xx

Figure 3.7 Assessment tool with criteria at different levels (/Wag-06/)

Wagner adds that the supplier is confronted by much higher requirements from the buyer's side, than this business is regularly required to fulfill. So the root-cause for buyer supplier relationships is often to be found "in the lacking experience and missing understanding of the perception of the business partner on both sides". For this reason, the assessment should not include only the business structure and its processes but also weigh the company culture and the mutual understanding (/Wag-06/).

3.1.2.4 Stage 4: Supplier Improvement planning & Cooperation agreement

In stage 4 a supplier improvement plan including the duties of both companies has to be formulated. The creation of a roadmap is recommended in order to coordinate and ratify the activities of the two organizations. The most important capabilities like quality, stable delivery and right prices are prioritized for the fast achievement of a minimum level of the demanded competency (/Fle-06/).

Based on the foregoing results from the supplier-audit, from the risk-assessment (described in stage 6) and the product-specifications the required changes at the supplier's site can be derived. The challenge to face is to combine the different findings in a way, so that the resulting improvement plan is based on objective decisions and includes all the important factors from the different findings, and, which is communicable and understandable by the supplier, who eventually has to agree on it or even execute the improvement leading to fundamental changes in its business. Once the supplier and the buyer agree on the future plan, a cooperation contract is worked out and has to be ratified. Optimally, this cooperation contract describes in detail the future procedures (action plans), requirements (like capacities and commitments) for improvement, and the measurement of progress showing the attained benefits. If there is a certain method (like the later presented XBSC, or the conducted approach) to be applied by both parties, this has also to be considered and fixed within the contract, as Kaufmann (/Kau-04/) states.

3.1.2.5 Stage 5: Technical supplier support planning / Supplier Improvement Support

In stage 5 the substantial improvement of the supplier's capabilities starts. This process persists for the entire period of supplier-buyer relationship. After the first main improvement of capabilities it might be referred to as supplier monitoring or supplier controlling (/Fle-06/); however, it may also be referred to as continuous buyer supplier relationship improvement. This stage describes all activities, which seek for improvement of the relationship in terms of quality, efficiency and thus benefits. Ideally, this improvement leads to a strategic long term partnership with both companies benefiting from the synergies, low waste and risks, and mutual cooperation and growth.

When planning the technical support in advance (in contrast to a reactive technical support) a reasonable effort for critical issues has to be defined by buyer and supplier, and the timeline of execution fixed. The technical supplier support has to be planned individually, since every problem or deficient process needs an individual approach and involvement. Kaplan and Norton (/Kap-04/ p. 7) explain that strategy maps can be used dynamically to design action plans by aligning the strategy map to the Balanced Scorecard. This sets up a basis for time/action plan connected cause- and effect-relationship visualization.

3.1.2.6 Stage 6: Risk-Assessment

Since the supplier assessment aims to identify the suppliers' capabilities and to estimate possible bottlenecks, stage 3 is the crucial point regarding the supplier/buyer risk management. Therefore, at this point the risk assessment starts as well and has to be continued until the end of the proposed supplier improvement process. However, in order to approach the possible risks – actively and reactively – there is a need for a tool that helps to identify, evaluate and finally prevent risks. Therefore, Fleischer proposes the Risk-FMEA method, which is presented in chapter 3.1.3 (/Fle-06/).

When developing a supplier in China, risks are evidently higher than in the home market: high project costs, only few business connections and no experience in the new market are only few elementary factors causing the risks to rise. Regarding the relationship between an IC buyer and a Chinese supplier, there are many risks emerging from the different cultures, languages, strategies, capabilities, and requirements etc. of both parties.

3.1.2.7 Stage 7: Supplier Improvement

This stage represents the supplier's activities to improve the supply performance and the quality of the relationship. However, the supplier's commitment to improvement is dependent on various factors, since it requires an investment first. Therefore, Patterson (/Pat-00/) states that suppliers have to be convinced of the direct benefits to its manufacturing operation and the potential return on investment. Considering the small and medium-sized suppliers, which underlie a significant competitive pressure to reduce costs, Patterson suggests following: the supplier has to agree on the project, and the buyer has to share the investment/the work required. Further, the buyer must not be judgmental and the product price must not be the primary measure.

3.1.2.8 Conclusion on the presented approach

The presented supplier development process by Fleischer (/Fle-06/) is created for the specific issues in China, and thus, it is well suitable to be applied as basis for the supplier improvement process of Chinese suppliers. In addition, if the supplier is lacking capabilities, it has to fulfill the requirement to enable improvement in a quick way with a minimum level of effort and in joint cooperation. Since the supplier development process includes the risk assessment and the audit, the main steps to know the deficiencies are undertaken. Nevertheless, the product itself may be source for information on lacking capabilities (e.g. poor material quality shows insufficient control in the supplier's procurement). In order to consider it, the supplier improvement has to focus the most critical factors. Afterwards, the goal of a partnership has to be emphasized, considering the special local characteristics in China (chapter 4.4 and 2.4). This means, the supplier improvement has to be holistic, it has to be executed on basis of active involvement and trust, and it has to combine short and long term objectives.

The most critical issues can be insufficient capabilities, representing hindrances on the way to attainment of the supplied product (e.g. supplier's employees' level of education, lacking of quality control as part of the production process etc.). These issues do not differ from the issues to consider in an IC, although they are often in a lot worse condition. However, the risks are eminently higher than if sourcing in the home market (cp. "Stage 6" (/Fle-06/) and chapter 2.4.4). Roughly, it can be said, these risks can be of environmental nature or brought in from the supplier's side. The environmental risks are not considered in this work, since it can be assumed that the company has a reason to source from China and considers the environmental risks as tolerable. In contrast, the product- and supplier-related risks have to be influenced in order to attain savings with the sourcing from China. The next chapter discusses possible approaches of how these risks can be calculated, estimated, aligned to business processes and avoided by improvement.

3.1.3 Risk Assessment as part of the SD in China

Fleischer (/Fle-06/) discusses the topic risk assessment during the supplier development in China. Since the risk evaluation is one of the key factors of supplier development, risks are defined as a future development or event that might adversely impact the achievement of corporate goals. For example, the event may lead to a lower profit or even cause the failure of a company. The in-depth interviews with purchasing professionals indicated that most companies made some sort of risk assessment, either formally or informally, but the majority of the persons interviewed recognized that, according to its relevance for the buying organization, there is a lack of supply risk management (/Fle-06/). Therefore, three approaches for risk assessment are presented in the following. The third approach by Fleischer (/Fle-06/) may be the most suitable one for the supplier development and improvement process in China.

3.1.3.1 Financially tangible approach

An approach of risk measurement is undertaken in a study by Zsidisin (2001) based on a case study from the communication and information industry. In this study, the evaluation of the supply risks is done by evaluating all commodities for their impact on the Earnings Before Interest and Taxes (EBIT), thus all purchased items are being analyzed for their potential to affect EBIT. The estimated impact on EBIT for each item was derived by quantifying the probabilities of the occurrence of different scenarios. Furthermore, measures and activities in order to avoid risks for each supplier are listed. The advantage of this supply-risk-measurement is the quantification of the impact of the possible risks in financial terms. Hence, it supports communication to top management and facilitates planning for the next fiscal year (/Fle-06/).

3.1.3.2 Risk management cycle

A second approach is the concept of risk management by Wildemann (2006), which shows the four main elements of the risk-management-cycle: risk identification (1), risk assessment and risk analysis (2), risk measures (3) and, risk control (4) in a closed loop. This cycle has to be repeated by the buying organization up to a suitable detail on all relevant divisions and functions of the company. In addition, Wildemann (2006) describes multiple strategies of action to lower the appeared risks. The Failure Modes and Effects Analysis (FMEA) method is a systematic and structured study of potential failures/risks that might occur in any part of a system to determine the probable operational success, with the aim of improvement in design, product and process development (British Standard Institute 1991). After the identification of all possible failure modes (or risks) in a further step a rating scale is used to assess the severity (1) of each factor, its chance of occurrence (2) and the likelihood of its detection (3). The multiplication of these three figures makes the Risk Priority Number (RPN) which is used for prioritizing the different failures modes (or risks). Hence, in a FMEA-near process Wildemann (2006) prioritizes the measures of interest: First, it is determined whether the actual RPN is acceptable. If this is not the case the relation between costs and impacts of the probable measures has to be deduced for finally choosing the best fitting one (/Fle-06/).

3.1.3.3 Current approach: Risk FMEA (/Fle-06/)

The third presented approach by Fleischer (/Fle-06/) aspires to combine the advantages of both presented risk assessment methods to attain an overall risk assessment suitable for the risk assessment within the supplier development:

The method presented is based on a risk assessment method in the product development, the "Failure Modes and Effects Analysis (FMEA)". It is used to cut costs by risks by decreasing the number of product failures. This goal can also be followed regarding the risks occurring with a supplier, if it is applied as part of the supplier development in low-cost-countries. To make the method useful for this case, it requires certain adaptation. The adaptation required is described with the following four steps:

1. Preliminary steps: First the examination of the boundary conditions is necessary. That regards to the definition of cost reduction targets, the purchasing volume, the assessment of the technical complexity and the country specific specialties. From there risks need to be identified that may occur during the purchasing project (/Fle-06/).

2. Rating scale for assessment: The standard FMEA rates the occurrence probability, severity and probability of detection. A scale from 1-10 is used while a lower degree describes a less important risk. The description of the rating scale needs to refer to the application

case. The severity of a risk for example mostly depends on when it would be discovered and the consequences (/Fle-06/).

3. Quantification scale: After the qualitative assessment of the occurrence probability, severity and probability of detection, their quantification follows. Therefore the occurrence probability is linked to a specific failure rate and the severity monetarily quantified in connection to the qualitative scale (/Fle-06/).

4. Result analysis: Normally the prioritization within the FMEA procedure is done by the Risk Priority Number (RPN) which is calculated through the multiplication of the occurrence probability, severity and probability of detection. Its values are between 1 and 1000. Now the quantification of the occurrence probability and the severity enables the calculation of the monetarily expressed risk height. It is defined as the risk height weighted by its occurrence probability. Ergo the calculation is possible through the multiplication of the occurrence probability and the severity. The advantage is that risk costs get considerable within the calculation of cost savings during a purchasing reorganization process (/Fle-06/).

First the possible risks within a procurement activity have to be identified. Cross functional teams are recommended for this task. The following categories of risk are proposed by Fleischer (/Fle-06/): "design, production, operational quality, purchasing, logistics, after-sales-service, management, finance and general risks". The country specific aspects have to be regarded carefully and included into the consideration of risks.

In step 2, the identified risks have to be assessed in the same team or preferably with experts. In order to quantify, three variables have to be evaluated: The probability of occurrence, the severity and the detection probability, which are assessed with a strict rating scale. The quantification can be done in figures from 1-10. The occurrence probability can be expressed in percent and the severity in a monetary value. From latter two figures, the "potential loss of money" (/Fle-06/) can be found by multiplication. The difficulty is to combine both hard and soft factors and to define their financial severity. Hard factors regularly can be expressed monetarily with little effort. However, soft factors need to be quantified monetarily as well to make them comparable. Therefore, this has regularly to be done by experts in the respective area.

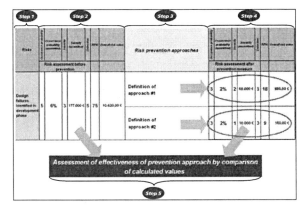

Figure 3.8 Steps of the Risk-FMEA (/Fle-06/)

The risks can be visualized differently for analysis. Since differing figures were used it is possible to rank the risks by their monetary value, and by their risk priority number (Figure 3.9). However, the monetary value is easier to discuss, since it is a tangible value. Another possible visualization is the representation of the risks in a risk map. There it is possible to describe the detection probability by the diameter, whereas the axis are occurrence probability and the monetary risk height.

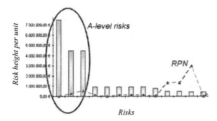 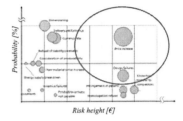

Figure 3.9 Risk height (/Fle-06/)   Figure 3.10 Risk Map (/Fle-06/)

In order to avoid the found risks, step 3 has to have risk prevention actions as result: they can reduce the severity, reduce the occurrence probability or increase the detection probability. Based on the identified risks, the organization, the supplier and the overall circumstances, the prevention approaches have to be designed by a cross functional team with highly experienced members. It is suggested to separate the teams for quantification and prevention finding in order to increase the objectivity and independent judgment. Regularly there are different possibilities to reduce the risks.

In the next step 4, it is required to repeat the quantification of risks in order to find out about the impact and whether the overall risks decrease as expected (analogous to step 2). Due to the dependencies between risks, this may be complex and problematic, and so, a difficult undertaking. Further, the caused costs by the risk sharing approaches need to be estimated, in order to calculate the return on invest.

In the last step 5, the approaches have to be selected based on the effectiveness and efficiency. It is recommended to integrate the expenses for risk sharing into the supplier development process, so that a "calculation of the real cost saving potential of a low-cost-supplier can be estimated (/Fle-06/).

3.1.3.4 Conclusion on the presented approach

The advantage of the presented Risk-FMEA calculation is the traceability of the risk causes and the monetary expression of the risks. Latter one is important, when discussing risks and deciding, which risks have to be prioritized and the ways to reduce them: (1) decrease the occurrence probability by implementing risk sharing initiatives, (2) reduce the (monetary) impact by changes of system or preparation, or (3) increase the probability of detection by control (e.g. in China a 100% goods receipt control is not an exception). So, the results from the risk assessment have to be included into the supplier development process to support the decision-making on the improvement respectively to be included in the improvement planning.

However, an open question is still the issue of aligning the initiatives to risks and deficiencies in order to find the most critical ones, which have to be improved quickly for the minimum required level of capabilities. With the "bridge" risk sharing initiative a risk can be connected to certain business processes (its non-availability or its lacking performance, which cause the risk). Upon an estimation, which processes are most critical, initiatives have to be implemented. It is required to find an approach, which embraces risks, deficiencies and products, and enables the communication of the issues between buyer and supplier.

3.1.4 Supplier Improvement as part of the supplier development

Companies are concentrating increasingly on their core competencies, so that the dependence of the supplier's performance and capabilities is growing. In order to stay competitive, the performance and capabilities have to be higher than the ones of the company's competitors. However, often the suppliers are lacking the fulfillment of these requirements. Thus, they have negative impact on "quality, delivery, cost reduction, financial health, adopting new technologies, and handling design changes" as Krause (/Kra-95/) states. In order to facilitate performance and capabilities companies apply the process of supplier improvement (/Kra-95/).

In the most literature supplier improvement is a bilateral effort by both the buying and supplying organizations to jointly improve the supplier's performance and/or capabilities in one or more of the following areas: "cost, quality, delivery, time-to-market, technology, environmental responsibility, managerial capability and financial viability" (/Fle-06/). When aiming for a long term relationship or partnership strong communication and interactions between supplier and buyer are required. Not only sales and procurement have to be involved, but a both sided cross-functional approach is recommended instead. This can lead to improvement of the supplier's capabilities in production and of the relationship, resulting in an enhanced overall performance. Further, the "active improvement of suppliers" is recommended by Soellner (/Soe-99/), which "requires a strong basis of trust, leading to long-term commitment on both sides". Min (/Min-98/) describes a best practice from a case study, where the management's goal is to improve a "quality control program by tracking supplier quality and delivery performance, establishing improvement targets in conjunction with suppliers, developing approaches to emphasize the partnership, and making it easier for suppliers to understand and satisfy the [*buyer's*] demanding quality requirements". In order to attain the best value for the final customers, the improvement activities have to go on in cooperative and continuous improvement efforts (/Von-99/).

3.1.4.1 Developing a world class supply base (/Kra-99/)

Krause and Handfield (/Kra-99/) present an overall supplier development process, which is meant to provide the stages and single steps from the identification of Supply Chain needs to the identification of suitable suppliers, which are being improved to meet production requirements. Further improvement makes the supplier a self-reliant supply base and finally leads to a globally aligned supplier network (see Figure 3.11). "Obviously, Krause and Handfield (/Kra-99/) have a higher objective than the supplier's fulfillment of the minimum requirements in order to attain a successful supply with this supplier improvement process" (/Fle-06/). For the minimum level of capabilities step 5 and 6 with the goal "Suppliers meet current production requirements" are the required steps.

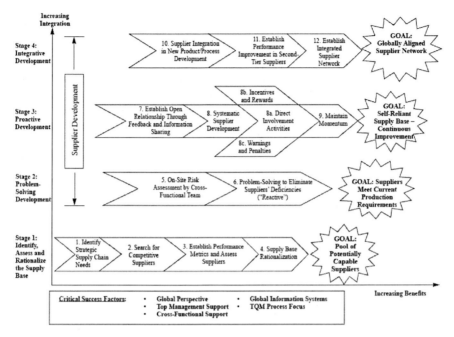

Figure 3.11 Supplier Development (/Kra-99/)

However, the processes leading to the "suppliers meet current production requirement" (stage "problem solving development" and later to the "self-reliant supply base" (stage "proactive development") meet the elementary needs of a supplier improvement process. First, the minimum level of capabilities has to be achieved and afterwards continuous supplier improvement applied.

The second stage "problem solving development" includes the assessment and the "reactive" solving of problems at the supplier's site. The in the risk-assessment process found supply risks and needs for improvement (in Fleischer's approach (/Flei-06/) these are separated actions) are the basis for an evaluation whether the supplier can meet future requirements. The assessment concentrates on all business processes responsible for the capabilities (chapter 3.1.2 "Audit"). In the next step, the problem solving strives for the mitigation of deficiencies: it is stated, that the preliminary established measurement system has to be used to give the supplier feedback on his performance and initiate discussions based on this facts.

In the case of a new supplier this should happen on the short term (first three to six months). Considering the results from the audit and the supply difficulties (quality and delivery), the essential processes to assure current production have to be focused first and long-term-problems postponed. Latter ones have to be managed later during the relationship. A presented case study suggests that in the case of critical problems, which the supplier cannot solve by himself, a buyer's team of specialists may support the supplier's employees. In order to execute such an initiative, there has to be a win-win situation between buyer and supplier, so that cooperation is fostered.

The third stage, "proactive development" is meant to be the ongoing/continuous improvement after the short-term objective "meeting the current production requirements" is attained: buyers who supported suppliers to achieve capabilities want to see their effort leading to growing benefits. However, following criteria are given as substantial to success: the supplied commodity is critical (cost, value, volume etc.), supplier has "systemic problems with cost, delivery or quality" and the management appears willing to cooperate. The presented approaches found from case studies can be categorized in direct involvement activities, declared incentives or rewards and warnings and penalties. It is concluded that in order to avoid regression of improvements, an ongoing appliance of latter or adapted approaches is required. The final integration part is not analyzed in consideration of this work's scope.

Handfield (/Han-00/ p. 4) explains that both firms need to commit "financial, capital, and personnel resources to work. Information has to be shared and a system to effectively and efficiently measure performance established. Hence, both companies are facing the challenge of trust into these activities: on the one hand the buyer's employees have to see the benefits (from working "for a supplier"); on the other hand the supplier has to follow the buyer's recommendations. Forker (/For-99/) emphasizes that misunderstandings of intent of the supplier improvement program will lead to low effectiveness. Such a problem can develop due to different understandings of priorities, motives, and methods. Therefore continual checks on the agreement are recommended ("either revising an ineffective program or enhancing understanding of an effective program"). Handfield concludes that success is even then not guaranteed, if both companies agree on and see the benefits of this attempt.

Conclusion

The reactive approach to improvement in step 6 is aimed at the weak points that require immediate actions for improving the supplier's capabilities to a minimum level, so that the supplier can meet production and/or service requirements (Kra-99/). However, how can risk and capability be evaluated and the progress measured jointly? Using a team of specialists to solve problems at the supplier's site is applied in China also, but without steady involvement the improvement is not lasting. An approach, which allows the measurement of progress and gives at the same time motivating objectives to the supplier, is required. Warnings and penalties can be referred to as passive involvement, since the buyer tries to push the supplier's effort by his power, without supporting actively. This approach is not recommended in China for orders with low volumes and high specialization, making the active involvement necessary. Further, it is mentioned (both desktop research and interviews) that the supplier has to understand the requirements and barriers, therefore the understanding has to be supported as well.

3.1.4.2 Occurring issues during supplier improvement (/Han-00/)

An improvement is in most cases well reasonable for both buyer and supplier. Though, problems and hindrances occurring on the way of execution have to be managed properly in order to attain a successful and lasting improvement. Handfield describes following issues and gives suggestions on it (/Han-00/ p. 6-16):

- Lack of Supplier Commitment: If the supplier's management is not convinced by the benefits resulting from improvement, it can't be successful or lasting. Potential rewards for the supplier's organization have to be clearly defined: e.g. by showing competitors performance development or by reducing order if no improvement is achieved. The executive commitment can be facilitated by letting managers see the direct increase of profit during the improvement activities (proper measures)

- Insufficient Supplier Resources: If the supplier lacks in capacities or capabilities the improvement activities require simplification in the first case. Further, the supplier can be supported actively by trainings (e.g. kaizen events), information in time and direct employee support by sending the buyer's engineers to the supplier's site.

- Lack of trust: In order to have a free sharing of information (required to a certain extend) intimidating legal issues and ineffective lines of communication need to be avoided and confidential information kept exclusive. Many companies require nondisclosure agreements and even exclusivity agreements. However, legal involvement ought to be on a low level.

Conclusion on occurring issues

From the presented occurring issues all occur with Chinese suppliers as well. In addition, China specific issues occur (which were mentioned in chapter 2.4.4 and are presented in chapter 4). However, the improvement is not a single change to execute. In contrast, it is a long-term process, which needs the motivation and support from both companies. Clear goals and objectives have to be aligned to measures in order to follow the progress of improvement. The required approach has to be fitted into the overall supplier development process and enable a structured and successful supplier improvement in China.

3.1.4.3 Process oriented Supplier Improvement (/Har-97/)

Hartley and Jones (/Har-97/) see the result-oriented supplier improvement lacking lastingness, because the suppliers are not capable to execute ongoing improvement. In their approach, Hartley and Jones introduce the process oriented supplier improvement. Based on change management, it has the advantage that the supplier's capabilities to provide changes without the buyer are facilitated.

Main characteristics of result-oriented improvement are:

(1) Standardized and buyer driven improvement process: the supplier has little influence on the changes made. The buyer analyzes the actual process, identifies problems and solves them.

(2) Changes made are of technical nature: therefore, the improvement does not consider differing culture, objectives and resources (which can have impact on the supplier's business).

(3) Process has a short duration and is not dependent on follow up: the buyer's team has knowledge in solving this kind of problems, so it conducts the problem solving and the initiatives to undertake. This leads to a fast attainment of goals, but the supplier's learning is limited.

Therefore, Hartley and Jones suggest that this result-oriented improvement has to be supported and accompanied by parallel changes in the supplier's social and managerial systems. Since these changes go deeply into the company's (and also employees') culture they take more time and require higher effort. As result however, the adaptation of continuous improvement initiatives and of the buyer's (quality, company) culture can be increased. Supplier's employees "learn how to identify and implement their own process improvements" (/Har-97/).

Conclusion on process oriented Supplier Improvement

As it is a complement to the result-oriented improvement, it can uncover synergies when improving the supplier's processes. Not lasting improvements have a lacking of effectiveness. Once made improvements are needed to persist. Especially in China (compare chapter 4), the transfer of not only know-how but also the understanding and the quality culture are suggested. Therefore, the aims recommended by Hartley and Jones count also for the China specific supplier improvement. The approach to conduct has to include the advantage of supporting lasting improvement (both on short and long term), the supplier's understanding, adapt to the required "culture", and have impact on the processes.

3.1.5 Supplier Improvement in China

A buyer, who attempts to improve the performance and capabilities, or the buyer supplier relationship itself, experiences problems regularly. Further, specific local characteristics have to be considered in order to succeed with the effort undertaken in China. As mentioned, the risks need stronger consideration, besides of the found deficits in the supplier's processes and the dissatisfactions of the supplied product. In addition to these product-related issues the relationship-related characteristics need to be paid more attention to (e.g. culture, strategy, quality of cooperation etc.; described in chapter 2.4.4 and 4).

Interviews and surveys conducted among German and Chinese companies have the aim to identify the most critical issues, the drivers of success and the experiences made. In the following an overview over the today's supplier improvement is given from the gathered data.

In view of the above shown problems and risks, it is reasonable that companies emphasize particular departments. Following to quality assurance, production and logistics, which have the biggest impact on the fulfillment of the main specifications, the procurement plays an elementary role. The reason is that latter one takes in the risk of processing low material quality, which, if undetected, can lead to risks regarding the very critical product safety (compare presented risks in 2.4.4). The management/executive level is important, since it decides over the improvement activities, its proceeding and success, and has to manage the actions in right way.

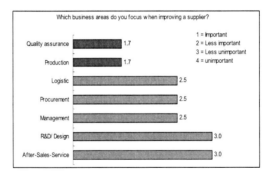

Figure 3.12 Graph showing the importance of business areas to focus

Today's companies consider the supplier development process, including the supplier improvement as a central element, and an important part of the operative, and partially even strategic, business. The applicability of these processes is strongly dependent on the company size, the country of application, the product to source and the suppliers. Since the improvement proceedings underlie a special pattern of characteristics on the Chinese market, an approach has to consider it in order to structure and enhance the required proceedings, resulting in the reduction of barriers and the increase of supportive elements. To enlarge the knowledge on supplier improvement in China, interviews including local companies were conducted. Further consideration of these characteristics is given in chapter 4.2 "Interviews with global playing companies in China".

3.2 Adapted BSCs for the Supply Chain Management

Since the prosperity of a buyer supplier relationship is dependent on both companies, respectively on the level of their satisfaction, both companies' goals have to be attended and aligned; otherwise lastingness hardly can be reached. Therefore, it is aspired to find a way to fulfill the requirements of the buying organization (which upon that can attain the savings), as well as the supplier's wishes (profit and order growth). A relationship is not tangible and can be described almost only in qualitative expressions. However, the relationship can be broken down into certain elements and partial processes, which make the basis for the "quality" of the resulting relationship. These processes can be improved. As "hard factors" may be the supplier's involved business processes that have direct impact on the supplied product or the risks for both companies; soft factors may be the shared/not shared information.

An approach based on the already mentioned Balanced Scorecard is well suited for the problems at hand. It enables the combination of objective and subjective (tangible and intangible) elements and to make these elements measurable. The measures in a BSC are both considering the past performance and are forward looking ("lagging and leading measures" cp. chapter 2.5.3). Thus, the BSC is not just a monitoring tool for a company, but also gives the possibility to plan changes in a long term strategy oriented way (/Cre-05/). For this case that would be a buyer supplier partnership that is profitable and prosperous for both parties.

Besides of long-term orientation, the short-term results have to be reviewed regularly, and, in the case of steady deficits, pushed or supported stronger to reach the given targets. So can e.g. the short-term profit, as one important goal for the supplier, be emphasized if required (e.g. to satisfy and motivate the supplier). However, also the short term results are achieved faster, because the cause and effects are planed beforehand, avoiding diverse initiatives to have negative impact on each other, thus saving time and effort.

3.2.1 Description of approaches

In the recent years the Supply Chain Management gained significance. The emerging Balanced Scorecard approach was found to be a possible tool to increase supply chain performance. Since the buyer supplier relationship may be seen as the "chain combining the links" in SCM, recent approaches are discussed in the following.

3.2.1.1 Supply Chain Performance Measurement

Ruggiero (/Rug-06/) describes the application of the Balanced Scorecard in the supply chain. The supply chain management is multiple-level task monitoring, and verifying the results and connections, so the BSC with its multiple perspectives is a well fitting method. Further, an advantage is that the measures proposed by this model are linked to the strategic goals and are therefore oriented to continuous improvement. A presented framework (originating from Brewer and Speh, 2000) aligns SCM-framework to the BSC perspectives.

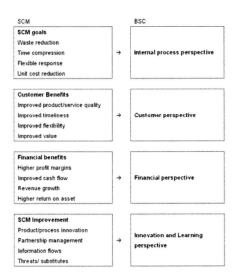

Figure 3.13 SCM Framework aligned to the BSC Perspectives (/Rug-06/)

Ruggiero concludes that there is a need for an extension with an inter-functional and inter-firm vision of performance in the internal processes perspective.

However, regarding the relationships between organizations as assets, they are not suited for being managed within the internal process perspectives for the reason of being intangible, and especially for a relationship between IC buyer and Chinese supplier require special attention. Therefore, many authors make further adaptations trying to integrate the characteristics occurring between the companies. For example, some approaches seek to manage this difficulty by adding a perspective: the cooperation (or collaboration) perspective.

3.2.1.2 Network Balanced Scorecard in the Supply Chain Controlling

Jehle (/Jeh-02/) introduces an adapted Balanced Scorecard as a possible tool in the Supply Chain Controlling. In Network Supply Chains organizations can benefit from knowing capabilities and needs of the supply-partners in redundant and long term relationships. Instead, there are often strong interdependencies in dynamic relationship, leading to the need for a new controlling approach. Based on that, the Balanced Scorecard was identified as a suitable tool due to its balanced appearance of management perspectives, and due to its popularity among today's companies.

The developed "Network Balanced Scorecard" includes basically the four original perspectives and in addition a fifth cooperation perspective. This perspective is meant to include and represent the cooperation relevant objectives, performance indicators and initiatives. Further, it makes the evaluation and the monitoring of a relationship possible. The financial perspective is as in the original approach the perspective of prime priority and includes the major strategy (e.g. cost reduction). Jehle concludes that an inter-organizational BSC requires an individual customization depending on the situation and stresses the dynamic usage of this method (regularly reviewing and adaptation of objectives).

3.2.1.3 SCM and the Balanced Scorecard

Similarly to the latter approach, Laschke (/Las-06/) states that a fifth perspective "collaboration" is necessary to measure the quality of the interactions between buyer and supplier and its competitiveness. This quality and competitiveness can be compared, if the according departments of the business(es) have similar key performance indicators (KPIs) (each of them have an own BSC). These KPIs do not have to be aggregateable to the superior BSC. Latter one's performance is represented by the strategic objective they belong to. Further Laschke points out, that there may be contradicting targets causing difficulties, when creating the KPIs in detail. For example a cost saving initiative in department one might increase costs in department two – these dependencies have to be considered. So, an approach like "reduction in dept. one" and at the same time "optimization in dept. two" may be a practical.

3.2.1.4 The BSC in Strategic Supplier Relationships

In the car manufacturing industry a company manages its key suppliers with the cross-Balanced Scorecard (X-BSC). Kaufmann (/Kau-04/) explains, the need for this approach comes from the multifaceted relationships requiring multidimensional measurement methods. Since each considered strategic supplier is different, an approach "tailored to the specific situation" is demanded. Traditional performance measurement could not fulfill the needs, since it was largely "over-engineered" in the case of non-strategic suppliers and for strategic ones not consistent enough. Further, the past indicators approach gave no possibility for forward looking, strategy-focused performance management.

So, the X-BSC is designed, which means to formulate and implement strategy for each relationship with a strategic supplier. Being the process owner, the buyer manages strategic partnerships and is therefore responsible for developing the X-BSC. However, the X-BSCs are the bridge between the buyer's and the supplier's regular BSC system. With this bridge the relationship has to be improved with a certain supplier relationship strategy. Benefits are considered to be: a powerful tool to manage strategic-supplier-relationships and decreased risks of delay. Since both parties are involved in planning and execution, the supplier is motivated for continuous improvement. The added transparency fosters fast and professional solutions of issues.

3.2.2 Deficits for improvement in China

The supplier management in China might be well supported by a Balanced Scorecard approach. Especially the combination of a strategic and operative supplier controlling tool within the BSC seems practical. The circumstances require a flexible method, with strategic orientation and short-term measurement, which preferably leads to short term results. However, neither was a contribution found on the topic "relationship/capability improvement with the BSC" in the contemporary research nor is one of the presented approaches satisfyingly suitable of solving the present local issues in China.

A Chinese supplier often represents a strategic supplier for the buyer, since following aspects appear: the sourcing from China often requires a high effort leading to high risks; buyers seek for a long term relationship respectively partnership; in this sector, the sourcing options are limited. The X-BSC presented by Kaufmann presupposes supplier's with high business capabilities and an already strong relationship between both companies, from which both are applying an internal BSC. However, the achieved benefits show the success and the sense of a BSC approach between two companies, as increase of efficiency, reliability and transparency and the decrease of risks, play an elementary role in China as well. However, the X-BSC does not include any cooperation perspective. This is reasonable since the relationship is already advanced and the cooperation is a "solid 'internal business process'". Similarly, within one company no cooperation perspective is needed because cooperation is expected. In contrast, in China this aspect has to be focused, as it is one of the critical ones (and probably even more due to cultural specialties).

The approaches by Laschke and Jehle integrate this perspective, but also not applicable for the case at hand. Jehle stresses that the presented approach focuses on heterarchic relationships, where both companies use their own Balanced Scorecards. It is mentioned briefly that a hierarchic appliance might be possible as well, but there is no solution presented. However, the main disadvantage of this concept is: this controlling tool shows the impacts of objectives of each company's BSC on the other company (buyer or supplier). But it embraces not, and thus, does not represent the relationship. So the relationship with its elements is not described, cannot be measured and also not be managed/improved with the BSC. The relationship requires one BSC, which is a strategic management tool for both organizations' mutual relationship. Laschke describes in a similarly oriented contribution how the BSC can help to control and compare the performance of different departments/levels. However, this approach does not consider the relationship as business factor, which, once improved by and for both companies, can help fulfill both companies' goals. In contrast, it is just integrated into the BSC's perspectives. Here, each department or company has its own Balanced Scorecards, not the relationship "has a BSC for itself".

Ruggiero's paper confirms the usability of the Balanced Scorecard for the supply chain performance measurement. With its multiple perspectives it can be a good support for continuous improvement. However, the problem of a BSC application inter-organizationally combining the strategic goals of two "independent" companies, or the relationship between them, remains.

4 Today's issues and practices of the Industry's Supplier Development in China

In order to learn more about the practices in supplier development and improvement and to understand the present problems of the sourcing in China, interviews with seven companies were executed. These interviews took place at companies in Germany and in China. Eventually, a survey rounded up the gathering of practical information.

In the following, the structure of the guidelines, the targets of the interviews and the attained information are presented. As the number of considered companies is not very high, the results can not be taken representatively for the industry of mechanical engineering of investment goods. However, the aim followed was to attain knowledge on the regularly occurring issues in business relationships in China. Since the interviews were accomplished with Germany based firms in Germany and China, they may show issues IC based companies regularly face when sourcing from Chinese suppliers. Furthermore, these issues are partially confirmed by the study from Salmi (/Sal-05/), who considered companies in Nordic Countries regarding a related topic.

4.1 Interviews with global playing companies in Germany

In the first part, three interviews in Germany and one interview in China were executed. The industry is mechanical engineering with focus on investment goods. The turnover of the companies interviewed was between ca. 100 Million - 4 Billion Euros. All companies have international experience and source in China.

4.1.1 Target definition

The interviews representing the first part had the aim to find out about the objectives followed with the procurement activity in China, about the management of Chinese suppliers, especially the supplier development process including the most relevant activities supplier assessment and improvement, and about the experiences (benefits and barriers) on the Chinese market.

4.1.2 Structure of the interview guideline

The guideline structure is divided into four parts. The first has the aim to get a general overview over the company interviewed and its activities in China. The second part has to identify the experiences made. Parts three and four focus the supplier assessment and the supplier development. In order to make the interviews comparable to reach a higher understanding of issues, the companies were asked about their company characteristics first. The size, turnover and the number of location sites play a big role considering the market power of the buying company; thus, it is also relevant for the supplier's standing. Further this section includes today's purchasing volumes, planned volume shifting and supplier structure, in order to understand the company's activities. To learn about the companies' experiences in China, problems with Chinese suppliers and the risk occurring are discussed. The third part of the interviews considers the supplier assessment in China. The questions attend the practices of investigation of capabilities and of specific specialties important for the Chinese market. The last section is devoted to the supplier development process. The information obtained gives insight into the development practices, its triggers and the benefits experienced. Last, the differences between IC and China are discussed.

4.1.3 Results

The interviews show that companies penetrated the Chinese market mainly to secure the market share due to the growing importance of the Chinese market on one side, on the other side the growing competition; due to the smaller distance geographically and culturally the East European market is seen to be in general more suitable for production of goods for the European market. However, the second most important reason is the low labor costs that result in lower production cost of locally produced products and in reduced costs of bought-in parts. The cost reduction is seen between 0% and 40% in comparison to German prices of bought-in parts. The third reason for sourcing in China, were the requirements brought by Local Content laws, which need to be fulfilled when selling on the Chinese market. None of the interviewed companies has extensive experience in managing Chinese suppliers, either because the short duration of presence and thus the experience period in the Chinese market or because the small ratio of sourcing volume there. As major drawback are mentioned the occurring risks, which reduce the potential savings eminently.

Each of the asked companies mentioned that both supplier development and improvement have a high and steadily increasing importance. The supplier improvement practices vary from a passive approach (request for improvement with the threat of rejection) to active involvement (with personnel supporting at the supplier's site). Depending on the market power of the company and the characteristics of its sourcing activity (complexity, order volume – now and future, size of the supplier etc.) the supplier improvement involvement is more or less active. The assessment process is realized in China to a great part by an audit, which takes in average about 12 working days while two audits are necessary regularly. If a company does not build up a production site in China, at least a purchasing department is established locally – local presence is, as all companies state, indispensable to achieve a successful supply. Regularly the companies use company-wide assessment tools and guidelines also in China. Regarding the supplier improvement, the active approaches are seen as flexible and situation-dependent ("fighting fires"). Rather passive approaches can be supported by a software tool, since it is more part of the general operative supplier management (e.g. monthly supplier self disclosure databases and measured performance). The budget for the supplier development or improvement is seldom being calculated a priori or in some cases not calculated at all. Further results were included into the conclusions.

4.2 Interviews with global playing companies in China

The second part of the interviews is represented by the three companies interviewed in China. They differ in size, their number of suppliers and also in the sourced lot-sizes and complexity of the sourced products. In order to enable a better understanding of barriers and benefits, not only investment goods companies were interviewed. However, mechanical engineering remained as constraint.

4.2.1 Target definition

The study sought to identify the triggers for supplier improvement, the applied practices, as well as the primary experiences made. In order to attain meaningful results, the companies were asked about their expectations on their supplier relationships, about their strategies in supplier management, and about the most critical elements of buyer supplier relationships in China.

4.2.2 Structure of the interview guideline

The interview guideline has six parts. In the beginning some elementary questions on the company allow a general overview. In the second part, the supply practices, the supplier structure and the major problems experienced during the sourcing are attended. In the following, the third part considers the supplier improvement from the buyer's point of view. Questions ask about supplier improvement practices, the strategy and the objectives of these operations, and whether the expected results are being reached. Further, information about the operative execution was of interest as well. In order to have a comparison to the supplier's aims, in part four the foregoing questions are complemented by information about the assumed supplier's strategy, his position towards improvement activities and the aims he strives for. The fifth part has the aim to learn about the key performance indicators buyers' use and the customs in supplier management/assessment. The closing questions ask for the fundamental standpoint towards the supplier improvement activities and the most critical point(s) of it.

4.2.3 Three case studies

In the following, three companies are presented as case studies. By this means, it is possible to compare the different approaches, the strategies and the barriers and benefits experienced. From that, the key elements of a successful supplier development in China are identified eventually. The following table gives a short overview over the companies' characteristics (the names were changed for anonymity reasons).

IC-Company*	Employees in China	Average Lotsize	CN-activity (years)	Complexity of Sourced parts	Supplier Improvement Involvement	Used KPIs	Cost drivers	Practices & Success
Chem Tech	12	1-5	1	Simple	Passive	Past	Time Effort	Result oriented discussion, mutual finding of problems in suppliers processes
Special-Mech	150	1-10	5	Simple Components Modules**	Active	Current	HR Time Effort	Cooperation, involvement in product finishing processes; strongly decreased rework-rate
Smart-Tool	180	50000	>10	Systems	Less Active for A-parts-suppliers	Past	HR Measuring	Audit resulting in suggestions and stimulation to change: "what should be changed why"

Overview over Characteristics of presented companies * Names changed
** Future

Case-study (1): ChemTech

This company's production site in China was established to enhance after-sales-services for local customers and the production of spare parts for the Chinese (and later German) market. For that and to leverage the low-labor costs, it is aiming for the development of suppliers and the suppliers' understanding for their products on the longer term. It is developing and producing specialized mechanical systems for the chemistry industry. Parts are safety-relevant so that quality has highest priority. Standing at the beginning of its China-activity, it is facing the above mentioned problems.

The aspired integration of suppliers on the long-term has advantages for both supplier and ChemTech: the supplier can learn, grow and increase the efficiency of production and cooperation; the buyer has a higher reliability, fulfilled requirement and an efficient supplier management. By applying this mutually beneficial strategy prospering relationships are expected. Supportingly, the firm has no rigorous cost-saving-plans; the highest objective is quality and delivery reliability. The maximum price to pay is the German supplier's one less the expenses caused through the supply from China. The so created buffer can be used to pay supplier-bonuses for good (quality-) achievements.

Nonetheless, it experiences almost always problems with quality within the first supply, so that parts are returned frequently. Since this Chinese location has overall only 12 employees it has limited resources to support and improve the suppliers. Besides of that, the buyer is cautious with transfer of know-how. Hence it awaits the fulfillment of the order. When the opposite case emerges personal discussions with the supplier follow to find the root-cause and to explain why another approach is required. A further past-indicators method used in this company is a technical scorecard, which aims for finding the root-causes as well: it visualizes the disparity between measured data at the supplier's and the buyer's site. Afterwards, a reworked or new batch is supplied – usually delivered in proper quality making further claims unnecessary. This shows that the capability to produce proper goods is available.

Especially for the specialized companies with small volumes supplier's short-term profit orientation represents a barrier, as they seek for the development of a long-term partnership with a learning-process first. In this case two major supplier's-strategies were encountered: On the one hand suppliers, which are cooperative and motivated to learn, which often the case is if they want to expand by increasing business with IC companies. On the other hand, suppliers with no deeper interest in cooperation, because the order represents only a small part of the supplier's business and seems to be considered "not worth the effort". Deemed to have its root cause in this fast changing market, the building of relationships is considered to be difficult, so that for certain parts in-sourcing is considered.

Case-study (2): SpecialMech

SpecialMech is an assembly site, which started its business in China five years ago. It sources all components to assemble them to finalized products. These investment goods are made-to-order for industry and require "German Quality" at low costs. Starting similarly to ChemTech five years ago, it confirms the experience of receiving poor quality from its suppliers in the beginning of the company's procurement activities. Since all parts are being purchased, this company needed to become involved strongly into supplier development and improvement. It sources mainly from medium-sized suppliers (from 51 up to 250 employees), including standardized and customer-specific parts. In the near future it is desired to implement the sourcing of modules.

With its strategy SpecialMech tries to create a long-term relationship with stable fulfillment of requirements. It experienced a rapid increase of quality, when suppliers understood the improvement to have direct impact on profit (stable growing orders, efficiency). Close cooperation and stimulation of understanding of the buyer's requirements emerged to be important factors leading to a successful relationship. A support team has the aim to improve the suppliers. In the case of small supplier companies (<50 employees) it is required to find out a reasonable way of how to solve issues and to explain the benefits, since it would be counterproductive if the feeling of being dictated emerged in the supplier's employees (supposed the supplier is not dependent on the buyer).

By investing HR-capacities and a lot of time in supplier management SpecialMech created the today's supplier management system: In the beginning of each relationship an explanation is given to the supplier, why improvement and the cooperation are beneficial. It is attempted to give the supplier an understanding of the WHY quality is required and HOW it can be attained. Engineering teams conduct site visits, are involved in finishing processes and educate and work together with suppliers' employees, whilst keeping close contact to procurement managers. Site visits include feedback from the sales, as well as from the operating employees, who are responsible for the end-product. Costs and benefits are shared indirectly with the suppliers: Basing on successful improvement and stable relationship the orders grow on the supplier's side and SpecialMech can increase its savings by lowering supply from Germany.

Although SpecialMech is satisfied with its suppliers' ambitions to improve processes and to fulfill requirements, it has still issues with product-quality. The independent suppliers are not easy to change – it often is a slow and not lasting process: barriers can be low motivation to learn (from a foreign company) and the often changing employees. Cooperation and commitment is felt to depend on the size of the supplying company: the smaller the order is for the supplier the more it leads to lacking delivery reliability as the order is prioritized lower. In this case monitoring concepts like the monthly assessment of quality and delivery reliability and concepts measuring the yearly improvement are not useful, since no pressure can be exerted on the supplier.

Case-study (3): Smart Tool

Smart Tool is in contrast to the foregoing companies not dealing with investment goods; it regards itself rather a trading company than a manufacturer of machine tools. Basing on its know-how on machine tools and customer-preferences it orders and sources finalized end-products for the German market. The product-development is laid into the hands of suppliers with mass-production-capacities, as required. After several years of experience in China, this company is represented by approx. 180 employees at its location, which is responsible for quality- and supplier-management. The purchased volume grew rapidly in the recent years, requiring improvement of certain suppliers to stay competitive; most of them have a size ranging between 50 and 1000 employees.

When developing a new supplier, this company aims for a long-term relationship as well. It is important to be able to rely on the suppliers, since they supply finalized end-products for the German market and Smart Tool is committed to responsibility towards its customers. During the development process problems with quality are experienced very frequently. Resulting rework, which can be necessary over years (long warranty-times and big order volumes), can get costly, because the supplier can not carry the total warranty costs (in spite of the contractual agreement). Further, the reduction of rework can evidently save costs for both Smart Tool and its suppliers and thus legitimates supplier improvement. In the opinion of Smart Tool's managers, a close cooperation is fundamental for supplier improvement, since personal contact is essential to assure discussed issues are completely understood.

Supplier improvement plays an increasingly important role, since occurring problems have direct impact on both supplier (liability) and Smart Tool (customers). The formerly used approach was a quality inspection, which checked the products and sent them to rework, if necessary. This method was very expensive in view of the big volume and the rework whilst the delivery date is near. A new approach includes an ABC analysis showing the most value generating suppliers. With these suppliers, a process-audit is being executed by Smart Tool or in depth by a third party, which finally results in a report. This report includes suggestions on improvement of the supplier's efficiency. In the future, the process-audit with its steps will be triggered additionally, when suppliers are constantly not fulfilling requirements and when suppliers have poor performance in comparison to their competitors. This way both companies can save costs and increase the orders.

Experience proves the supplier improvement not lasting if not constantly monitored. Further, the present interest of the suppliers to improve is confronted by the short-term profit orientation. Latter one can be approached by declaring and visualizing the direct losses, which decrease the short-term profit, and convincing the suppliers, so that they become willing and eager to learn and to fulfill stable quality. Smart Tool believes that this target is reachable in the future: suppliers can do well if the buyer is helpful enough by providing the needed support and knowledge in the right way.

4.2.4 Results

Since the companies interviewed differ strongly, the results are not directly comparable, but certain similarities exist even though. Each company stated that the beginning of sourcing in China goes hand in hand with problems in quality, delivery reliability and difficulties regarding the cooperation with Chinese suppliers. But, it was stated further that it is (will be) possible to override these problems. So, the problems are considered to be manageable making sourcing in China successful and prosperous, based on certain approaches and actions.

Because the supplier can increase his profit producing many parts of the same kind, and even better if there is only little preparation-work necessary, he strives for orders fulfilling these conditions. If they are not given, supplier's try to fulfill the order without investing the necessary energy and commitment, leading to non-fulfillment of requirements.

However, specialized parts in small volumes and comparatively good reliability and quality can be achieved yet. This may be connected to a well-known name and the expected order-growth, but the achievements are mainly attained by active involvement practices: the share of know-how in production processes, the education in quality and the regularly motivated feedback. The active monitoring stimulates the supplier to share information in time. It was also considered important that suppliers have to learn that efficiency and long-term orientation influence also the short-term profit positively, instead of diminishing it (e.g. decreased rework in 1st order saves profit-loss directly).

IC buyers in China are long term oriented; in contrast, the supplier thinks operatively and rather on the shorter term. The buyers see the need for convincing the supplier on the topic of supplier improvement, with profit as main argument: "less waste, higher profit". Also incentives as "growing orders" and "better standing towards international companies" can be used. However, every short term benefit (turning directly into profit) has typically a strong impact. Naturally, the size of the buying company and the outlook to orders play a role. But, besides of the short term orientation, the basic willingness to learn is considered to be available.

Besides of the quality and delivery reliability, often mentioned problems are material-related. It was stated that the suppliers themselves might have well working business processes but the 2nd or 3rd tier suppliers bring in materials which do not fulfill requirements or delay delivery, resulting in poor performance.

Cost drivers of the supplier development and improvement are always the increased effort in comparison to activities in IC. Both passive and active involvement need HR-capacities (whereat the active one of course more). As another major cost driver, was mentioned the invested time (supplier management, supplier development and improvement, to attain a successful supply etc.), which decreases the capacity and efficiency.

Databases to support future improvements with certain approaches and solutions found in the past are not in use or planned, since the supplier-improvement is considered to be dynamic and flexible. Each problem is approached and solved individually. In the case of the strong active involvement, the supplier improvement and -development teams are often regarded to be experts in their activities. Also methods and concepts are not applied within these processes, the expertise and negotiation is the driver of success. Only in few cases, e.g. often occurring safety issues, which need a similar proceeding to avoid them, there are used templates to manage these issues safely and fast.

4.3 Survey in Germany

The information found in the interviews was extended by a survey conducted under German companies with sourcing activities in China. The aim of the survey was to get more information about the China-sourcing activities, the expectations, the approaches applied and the risks occurring. The results are of numerical nature, so that they were used for diagrams in chapter 2.4.4 and 3.1.5. Further findings were used for the validation of the beforehand found results.

4.4 Requirements for BS-Relationship Improvement in China

Strategy in China

Once the management decides the strategic step to source in China, many extraordinary topics have to be considered. Special attention has to be given to the monitoring, since this assures the fulfillment of requirements and because the OEM has to rely on the supplier. In China relying without monitoring can become very costly for the buyer, due to the high project cost and commitments towards the final customer. For the smaller companies due to increased dependency even critical. It is recommended to connect monitoring as soon as possible to the supplier's processes and begin in the best case in the supplier's procurement to assure proper material quality.

Active vs. Passive Involvement

Both active and passive involvements are applied in China. The passive involvement is more suitable for relationships, which may need improvement in the sense of efficiency and optimization, but the supply is already stable. However, even the passive involvement requires a higher effort in China than in the home market, since rework issues and complaints occurred more often. Regarding relationships with essential problems in quality- and delivery-reliability, especially for the specialized industry with low-volume-orders, the passive involvement is not recommended.

In contrast, the active involvement tries to boost the supplier on a minimum level of capabilities in order to attain a successful supply. Involvement means gathering information about the supplier's processes, so that a better risk-calculation and earlier intervention are possible, resulting further in enhanced learning by the supplier. However, when the buyer is actively involved into the processes, he can monitor the supplier. The buyer can get feedback from different company levels, for example from the production enabling him to make himself a picture of the progression of his order.

Naturally (improvement) activities cause primarily higher expenses than passive performance measurement and reporting. Though, especially for the procurement in China, the strategic and operative monitoring of the suppliers is a powerful approach enabling sourcing with savings for the buyer and reduced rework as direct benefit for the supplier. Followed on the longer term, the achieved reliability can be lasting. This is especially for the considered industry an important achievement.

Current Indicators vs. Past Indicators

Using past indicators is common, as it is the classic cause for passive involvement. It is easy measurable and clearly communicable with the suppliers (e.g. percentage of delivery in time or number of quality complaints in the last month). The problem about past indicators is that they capture only past deliveries so that they don't express anything about the current situation at the supplier's site, about the responsible causes or the development in the future.

For the considered industry in China, an approach is required, which enables to monitor the current situation, in order to intervene before it is too late and costs rise for both buyer and supplier. E.g. to monitor the production process an order-processing-schedule could be defined, which would be reviewed periodically during the order-processing: irregularities showing attention-requiring issues could be solved in time to assure a successful delivery.

Personal involvement

Each of the interviewed companies stated that personal involvement is indispensable for building a relationship with a Chinese supplier. Even Smart Tool, which has a considerable market-power, prioritizes personal contact, as it is essential to assure that the supplier's managers understand the ideas behind suggestions, to explain why and how the supplier benefits from improvement: "direct loss of money" is well understood, and thus process consultancy normally appreciated.

Further, the tracking of the production is suggested. The earlier the buyer knows about problems the lower are the correction costs – in contrast the worst case is when all parts are produced and delivered, and have to be reworked ex post. To avoid latter issue, procurement staff has to consider discussing with the involved supplier's employees in order to get feedback on present issues and to "educate" them in terms of quality and priority; agreements and incentives can be motivating for the supplier.

The buyer can take advantage of the local culture, which allows discussing different issues and enhance the monitoring. In comparison to IC companies Chinese companies are open to showing certain company areas: they demonstrate willingness to share information (e.g. tour through the production line – even competitors). On the other hand, problems are discussed less openly as it means "losing the face". Thus, problems at supplier's processes require to be approached cautiously by a skilful negotiator of the supplier improvement team.

Finding the right ratio

The presented kinds of involvement are naturally never unilateral in reality. A big challenge is to find the right ratio of active and passive involvement. Due to many influencing factors it has to be decided, as the case arises.

However, as fundamental orientation the activity oriented is the less risky strategy resulting in faster growth of stable fulfillment of requirements. Not only because the supplier can be improved in a short time, it also enables the continuous monitoring, which is essential in China to have a lasting prosperous and successful relationship.

5 Requirements for the BSC approach in brief

"Chinese suppliers require steady and an extensive and in-depth control-mechanism" a consultant of the Hong Kong Trade Development Council explained to the author of this work. This was also confirmed by the findings in the interviews, where it was stated that a 100% goods-receive-control partially is required. This may be caused by the suppliers' company culture or the "full order books", making them not dependent on one buyer. Another statement from the interviews had the thought that it may also be caused by the highly dynamic and rising market, so that the companies concentrate on orders/profit, often without long term orientation or strategy. This naturally differs essentially from the orientation of an IC company establishing a production facility or a supply base in China and undertaking the effort to improve its suppliers. These differing strategies require alignment, both suppliers and buyers aims have to be balanced; a win-win situation has to be created.

Literature investigation found no structured approach, which presents a guideline to improve a Chinese supplier. The methods used in the industry are regularly the same as in IC. However, some companies realized that the suppliers in China need special attention in order to establish successful sourcing, also without high market power (big sourcing volumes, which, if present, are evidently advantageous). These "best-practices" have to be combined in a framework, which supports the fulfillment of the requirements of a buyer supplier relationship in China. So, hindrances and barriers for the improvement of capabilities need to be lowered in the first case, and enable the buyer and the supplier to reach their goals.

Supplier Development

The supplier development process presented in the desktop research by Fleischer (/Fle-06/) is considering China specific requirements. It includes the preliminary steps to the risk assessment, the specific assessment system and the following supplier improvement planning and improvement execution. However, no detailed description of this planning and a possible and structured execution between an IC buyer and a Chinese supplier is given. This gives room for further research, to which attention is paid in the next chapter.

Supplier Improvement

The buyer driven supplier improvement process itself is from the 1990's on considered in research. There, issues were uncovered and suggestions given of how to solve them. Most of these issues and problems are applicable for the improvement activities of a Chinese supplier, and thus, have to be considered if designing a concept to support improvement. However, the lacking of consideration of a relationship between an IC buyer and Chinese supplier represents a research gap. The found issues and best practices in the interviews suggest an active involvement to foster understanding and the application of past and current indicators in order to see the progress and development. Furthermore, the ability to intervene in time, a strong personal involvement, a right proportion of active support and passive monitoring can be facilitated this way. Last, in order to make increase the final value of the effort, lastingness requires to be supported and continuous improvement realized, by educating the supplier regarding the topics "continuous improvement".

6 BSC-based Relationship Improvement as part of the Supplier Development in China

The introduction of the Balanced Scorecard (BSC) by Kaplan and Norton in the year 1996 was the basis for its appliance in different companies, where adaptations were conducted to fit the BSCs to their business structures and ideas. Within the years of use, the BSC approach was underlying an ongoing transformation and finally resulted in the alignment with the strategy maps in the year 2004 (/Cre-05/ p.2).

As shown (cp. chapter 3.2), research and industry present approaches on an inter-organizational and co-operational Balanced Scorecard. Each of these approaches was created to fit a certain area in the supply management. However, the approaches do not meet the requirements at hand that occur when improving a newly founded buyer supplier relationship. Also the improvement aspects are not properly solved for the given situation in China.

Therefore, the Balanced Scorecard approach in this work strives for the consideration of the China specific requirements of a relationship, based on the interviews and research. This relationship can be regarded as an insubstantial entity of both companies, which is formed by the involved employees, and the material and information transactions. Latter ones can be defined by single elements (e.g. culture, product, requirements, strategy and aims etc.), which need to be taken into consideration in order to develop and keep a prosperous relationship. For that reason, the BSC approach in this work has the aim to improve the relationship itself and, with this, ease the supplier improvement effort. When focusing on the enhancement of the relationship, synergetic effects, increased cooperation efficiency and reduced risks (leading to higher profit/savings) for both parties can be expected.

A specialty of this BSC approach is that it is driven by both companies at the same time and that it strives for aligning their strategies and aims, they apply this strategic management tool on the "joint asset" buyer supplier relationship. A true win-win situation has to be realized in order to create the basis for a long term cooperation beginning from zero. There are both tangible and intangible elements of the relationship, which need to be considered and improved, making the application of the BSC a promising approach (see chapter 3.2).

With the strategy maps as extending tool of the BSC it is possible to align the intangible assets with the tangible ones in a cause-and-effect connection, which supports the explanation and the understanding of why the sponsoring of not directly monetary objectives can be beneficial. From the superior BSC it is likely to create some lower BSCs in order to broaden the functional accessibility and operative relevancy. So, a capability improving BSC is developed, which embraces the results from the risk assessment and the executed supplier audit, and eventually the product characteristics, which give information on the real outcomes.

In the following chapters it is aspired to design a conceptual method enabling the buying IC company and the Chinese supplier to attain a successful supply with a win-win situation leading to a long term partnership – despite of the adverse conditions. In other words, the aim is to enhance and improve the buyer supplier relationship to achieve a competitive partnership with benefits for both companies.

6.1 Adaptation of the BSC

In this adapted Balanced Scorecard approach, the customer perspective is representing the buyer's requirements and wishes. This is fact, because in the considered buyer supplier relationship, the buyer represents, towards the supplier, the "final customer". Further, it can be said, that the buyer due to his commitment towards the final customer eventually represents latter one. Hence, this perspective includes the value the supplier is required to provide to the buyer: services and products at low cost with the demanded quality and better reliability than competitors, the supplier can increase his value by fostering a long term relationship. There against, the internal processes perspective focuses the supplier's business processes that are lacking capabilities. In this perspective, the assessment's results can be considered and the strategic orientation aligned to improvement. However, the four perspectives of the original Balanced Scorecard are considered not to be sufficient to embrace the intangible assets of a relationship, which are relevant drivers of success and prospect. Therefore, the fifth perspective "cooperation", presented in chapter 3.2, is adopted in this approach.

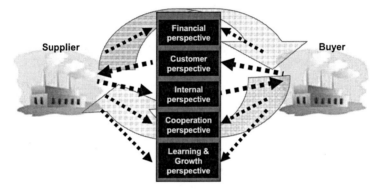

Figure 6.1 BSC based Buyer Supplier Relationship Improvement

In contrast to Kaufmann's X-BSC (/Kau-04/; presented in chapter 3.2.1) the companies are not mutually involved in an already long time lasting relationship. The relationship between an IC buyer and a Chinese supplier is just in the beginning. Therefore, the cooperation perspective is added – the cooperation is naturally influenced by both parties. Here, the BSC does not combine two existing BSCs, but it considers the relationship as an entity to improve. This relationship includes the buyer's requirements in the customer perspective and the supplier's processes in the internal process perspective. The other perspectives reach for a mutually beneficial goal, in other words, a win-win situation. This is necessary for this BSC to be successful. Therefore, the financial perspective includes the objectives growth and productivity. Productivity means the increase of efficiency for both buyer and supplier; growth includes the increase of profit and savings. Accordingly, the learning and growth perspective is influenced by both buyer and supplier: the buyer can apply the gathered knowledge at other suppliers' sites, improve his Guanxi and relationship to the supplier's employees and use this network for lasting improvement. The supplier on the other side gets "free" consultancy regarding his processes that are lacking performance. Naturally, this requires effort in the beginning, but eventually the supplier can improve, leading to higher profit; lasting knowledge enables him to improve continuously and increase his competitiveness towards Chinese (and IC) suppliers.

6.1.1 Cooperation perspective

As in some of the presented approaches (cp. chapter 3.2), the cooperation perspective is for the buyer supplier relationship in China an important extension of the original Balanced Scorecard. The interviews show that in China the personal contact, the nature of relation and cooperation and the communication are not matter of course. The cooperation perspective includes the strategic objectives attending to the issues, which are not directly impacting the product and productivity or the profit and savings. But, they are the basis for a prosperous relationship in China, as employees are the basis for learning and growth for both companies.

The strategic objectives placed in the cooperation perspective represent the elements of the relationship that strengthen, stabilize and grow the relationship. It is aspired to form the basis for a better understanding between the Chinese supplier and the IC buyer. The Chinese supplier can see why capacities (HR, time, finance) need to be jointly invested into the relationship, and how this finally can lead to benefits.

Thus, the Balanced Scorecard can visualize all cooperation relevant objectives, measures and initiatives. It makes possible to see the resulting effect on the other – tangible – objectives. For that reason, the cooperation perspective assures that the cooperation/relationship relevant aspects are linked to the overall strategy. In order to make this perspective practical, the objectives have to be understood, be measurable and influenceable by initiatives. To foster understanding, the Strategy maps are a suitable approach. Further advantage results from the possible alignment to the BSC, and with that, the alignment to the action plan.

6.2 Improvement Strategy Maps

The interviews show that the strategic orientations of both companies involved differ in some areas leading to the need for a strategic alignment between both companies. Besides of that, the present communication problem needs consideration as well, in order to facilitate the process. The recently published approach "Strategy Maps" by Kaplan and Norton (/Kap-04/) are highly suitable to fulfill these requirements. They show the strategic objectives in a cause-and-effect relation and can be a great support for the communication of issues, helping to describe and explain the nature of present problems and the direct benefits resulting from their solution. The strategy map is the basis for the BSC, making it easier to understand the connection of an intangible asset (e.g. the "Supplier's understanding of the WHY to improve") to the increase of profit and savings. In the scope of this work, two Strategy maps are developed: the Buyer Supplier Relationship Improvement Strategy Map and the "Audit-Strategy Map". They differ in their aims and execution periods.

The Buyer Supplier Relationship Improvement Strategy Map has the goal for both companies to improve the relationship steadily, to show the strategic objectives in connection to the benefits (short and long term). These objectives have to be adapted with the time of appliance, since the objectives for continuous improvement change. The supposed period of use is from the beginning on continuously, also after the remedy of the critically deficient processes. In the supplier development process by Fleischer (/Fle-06/) it would be part of stage 5 (see Figure 3.5).

The "Audit-Strategy Map" is subordinated to the Buyer Supplier Relationship Improvement strategy. It describes the most critical goals to achieve to boost the supplier's capabilities in order to fulfill the minimum level of requirements. Therefore, it is meant to be used mostly in the beginning of the relationship. But it can also be continuously adapted and used over the whole relationship period. The main idea is to secure the first orders and the fast improvement of the most critical processes to stabilize and assure reliable supply as soon as possible. First, the basic requirements in terms of quality, technology, logistics or price and risks have to be met. Second, if the supplier is able to supply the product, he may still have certain problems, which need short-term improvement to minimize risk of unsatisfying quality or delivery reliability. In the supplier development process by Fleischer (/Fle-06/) it would be part of stage 7 (see Figure 3.5).

In both cases, the supplier may have problems to improve the deficient processes on his own. The "Audit-BSC" has the aim to support an active involvement from buyer's side, and thus a jointly conducted supplier improvement. Result of this improvement has to be a successful and for the beginning satisfying supply of the required products, and the foundation of a partnership-oriented business relationship.

6.2.1 Strategy maps as roadmaps to improvement

As shown in Fleischer's approach (/Fle-06/; see Figure 3.5) on supplier development process in China, after the decision to cooperate in a buyer supplier relationship, a roadmap for further proceedings has to be set up. This roadmap has to include the steps for supplier improvement to attain minimum requirements to meet current production. Today's industry seeks for long term relationships. This counts especially for the specialized mechanical engineering industry (e.g. made-to-order investment goods), which require further improvement. Therefore it is desired that the planning is aligned to long term orientation.

Strategy maps, visualize the long term goals to achieve and can include also the strategic objective of improving the supplier's capabilities. This objective can be prioritized in the beginning by e.g., giving it higher funding, without losing sight of the other relevant elements of the relationship. In this work, the strategy maps are the basis for the Balanced Scorecards, which transform the strategy into action (/Kap-04/), by aligning the objectives to measures (status / targets), and the initiatives/actions with resources to improve the status. The BSC also includes the deadlines for the attainment of the targets and the owners who are responsible for their achievement. Based on this information it is possible to establish a project plan with responsibilities, schedule and performance goals and given costs (see Figure 6.2). "This combined strategy map and Balanced Scorecard allows the effectiveness of the strategy to be constantly monitored and initiatives to be managed with the goal of closing any gaps between target performance and actual results" (/Kap-04/ p. 7). Hence, a roadmap/ projectplan/ actionplan including the major tasks can be designed. It includes budget and responsibilities for the actions to undertake aligned to a timeline with deadlines (resulting from the time-bound targets).

Figure 6.2 Illustration process to Projectplan for Improvement

6.2.2 Strategy map for Buyer Supplier Relationship Improvement

Creelman and Makhijani (/Cre-05/ p. 33) state that one of the Balanced Scorecard's strengths is its flexibility and adaptability, which has also led to wide interpretations and deployments. Since the improvement of a relationship has multiple levels, a proper strategy has to be found to reach the critical capabilities as soon as possible with a reasonable effort for both of the companies.

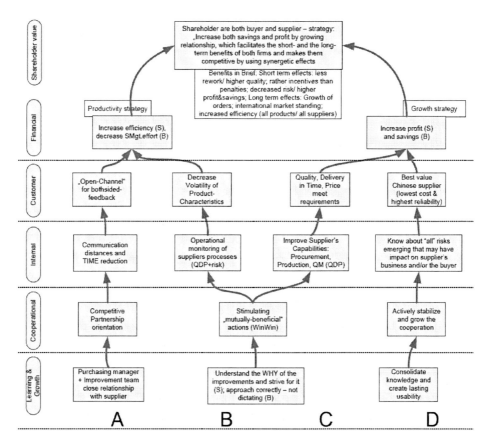

Figure 6.3 Buyer Supplier Relationship Improvement Strategy Map (themes)

The presented strategic objectives in the strategy map are based on the findings from the interviews presented in chapter 4 and the desktop research in chapter 3. The strategy, which needs to be followed in order to achieve the common and mutual goals, is defined as: „Increase both savings and profit by growing a relationship, which facilitates the short- and the long-term benefits of both companies and makes them competitive by using synergetic effects" (see Figure 6.3). The 16 included strategic objectives are explained in the following.

a) Learning and Growth perspective:

The purchasing manager, the actively involved improvement team, and the supplier's employees (management, production, procurement etc.) have to strive for a close buyer supplier relationship, since this supports, even enables a well working cooperation, as personal contact is highly important in China. The triangle of purchasing manager, the improvement team and the supplier's employees has to be close, in order to achieve meaningful and lasting results. The purchasing manager measures and supervises the current performance and the relationship. The improvement team executes the needed activities in cooperation with the supplier's strongly involved employees. These participants are required to have the same knowledge base, which leads to decisions made upon joint agreement and a mutual striving for the fulfillment of settled goals.

Understanding the reason for improvement has not to be limited to the management level. All employees have to learn the meaning of continuous improvement. Naturally, the motivation is a different one. Further, it is important that the employees clearly understand the reason for improvement, e.g. that there is a loss of profit on every inefficient day. This has to be achieved by a correct approach from the buyer's side so that the "supplier" gets convinced of the prosperity of this project.

To make the improvements lasting and usable for the supplier's employees, the transferred know-how has to be "translated" to the individual culture and maturity of the supplier. It is required to support the development of standards that are understood and applied by both supplier and buyer. Further, the lastingness of the future improvement is to be supported by developing the "thinking" (e.g. critical approaches to issues, quality awareness etc.) The buying company's traditions for products and processes, and the ones towards the final customers have to explained and introduced at the supplier's firm.

b) Cooperation perspective:

Competitive partnership orientation is a strategic objective, which is supported by having close personnel relationships. It has the aim of orienting the relationship not only to business goals (financially) but also to a longer term relationship, guaranteeing a stable and reliable cooperation in this dynamic market. This leads to enhanced efficiency and competitiveness in comparison to other business relationships by taking advantage of synergetic effects, information sharing and self-commitment.

By understanding the reasons making supplier improvement necessary, the supplier can improve his organization in whole. However, this engagement from buyer's side naturally expects commitment from supplier's side, which has to be motivated to dedicate personnel and time to the improvement process: measurement, initiatives and planning is necessary ("No pain, no gain"). Emphasis lies on "mutually" and "win-win": it means, actions having impact on the product or processes need preliminarily consultation with the other party to decrease risk of a sudden emerging problem. Furthermore, it supports the fact that a prosperous relationship is achievable only when both parties profit from it.

Research and interviews show that the active and personal involvement is more important in China than in the home market (the Guanxi specific issues as mentioned). Cultural, communication and understanding issues are hindrances, which need active and personal involvement. It is the buyer who pushes improvement, so he has to show active involvement. However, this is strongly dependent on characteristics like market power, order volume and product, company size etc. With increasing trust and capabilities the buyer has less risk and can give the supplier more responsibilities.

c) Internal processes perspective:

In the interviews "time" was presented repeatedly as major cost driver. This can be caused by the inefficient communication, the necessity to rework, the personal and active involvement, the time for feedback, the time for repeated checking, etc. The product related issues have to be solved by the improvement of processes, which is described in the next two paragraphs. Further, one issue here is the solution at the same time: By increasing active involvement up to a certain level it is possible to enhance the communication effectiveness and efficiency. The time for feedback gets reduced rapidly and the repeated checking can be decreased. Of course, the strong involvement requires time and effort, and hence also produces costs. But, costs can be saved by reduced risk, and the time by fewer misunderstandings, so action up to a suitable level is it.

The approach at hand seeks to improve the relationship, as well as the supplier itself. So it has to underlie certain actions and changes. But which changes to make? "People can't manage what they can't measure, and they can't measure what they can't describe" state Kaplan and Norton (/Kap-04/ p.3). Supported by the strategic objectives "understand WHY" and "win-win" this basis is given. The operational monitoring of the supplier's processes has to uncover the main risk- and inefficiency-causes. It is part of the subordinated Audit-Balanced Scorecard to measure the performance indicators, which serve with relevant information on: the supplier's business structure and processes, the operations impacting the product, and the improvement progress achieved. This monitoring decreases risk due to deeper insight into the processes and the enabled intervention in time. Another part of this monitoring is the measurement of all measures, which is required for the Balanced Scorecards use, because "performance measures serve as a fact-based vehicle for initiating discussions on specific areas that require immediate action and improvement" (/Han-99/ 34).

To boost the supplier's capabilities is the main goal after the audit and the risk-assessment uncovered the main deficiencies in the supplier's business structure and processes. Since this work emphasizes the improvement in the scope of the supplier development, this is one of the main parts. It is required that the supplier enhances these deficient processes in order to ensure a successful supply. Therefore, short-term effective initiatives decreasing the major risks have to be applied. Long term issues need to be reconsidered in the ongoing relationship. The production process has to be monitored and initiatives executed if required. It is suggested that the buyer is actively involved into this process to monitor and support the supplier to execute the accurate initiatives. This "boosting" of supplier's capabilities is emphasized with the Audit strategy map and the Audit-BSC.

With a stable and growing cooperation, the buyer and the supplier can find the risks that can be serious for the production. Therefore the supplier's processes impacting directly the product have to be known exactly regarding their risks (the risks found beforehand in the audit or the regular supplier development are not sufficiently covering). The supplier has to know and give feedback on issues, which may lead to risks. The buyer has obviously to do the same, since he would cause damage to himself if not sharing risks beforehand. Further, the risks imposed by the relationship can be crucial, since communication and feedback can be drivers of misunderstandings leading to unwished outcomes.

d) Customer perspective:

The "open channel" for feedback enables both sides to communicate openly. It is aspired to create a communication without barriers that is regularly experienced between companies, especially in new relationships in China. If an issue occurs it needs to be possible to discuss it. This discussion has always to be motivated, if it could have impact on the other party. With that, process-problems are discussed in time, suggestions made, and the monitoring and support coordinated. Both buyer and supplier benefit from in-time solutions so that requirements can be fulfilled as needed. For the buyer the created transparency means a reduction of risks, since he has the possibility to take influence.

The high volatility regularly experienced with bought-in parts represents a big problem for the buyer, since risk calculation, redundancy planning, and planning in general become complicated. So, one of the advantages of the operational monitoring is that the processes can be stabilized by taking action against the disturbing factors, like for example the bullwhip effect is (material is an often mentioned issue, so a stock for critical material could be built up).

The main characteristics of a competitive product are quality, delivery in time, and the price as required. By improving the processes and the relationship this target can be consequently achieved. Actually, the mentioned characteristics are the basic requirements to claim from a buyer supplier relationship. Since in China the processes are often not developed enough and employees lack know-how, these basic requirements have to be achieved first. So, the value for the customer is not only the supplied product itself (even if still the highest) but also the willingness for cooperation and mutual understanding. If this is given, the rework rate can sink, with the buyer sharing know-how, and processes getting improved. The reduction of rework rate has a direct benefit for the buyer, as well, as for the supplier, who attains a higher net profit.

When the supplier achieves not only the meeting of requirements but more than that, he can generate the best value for the buyer, assuring him the trust and the loyalty of this buyer. The best value can be described as "lowest cost & highest reliability". Of course, an ideal supplier is not attainable, but a supplier with an average IC performance at low cost as an average Chinese supplier is imaginable and highly interesting for an IC buyer.

e) Financial perspective:

The financial perspective is separated into two parts: The productivity strategy and the growth strategy. With the attainment of these strategic objectives, the shareholder value is reached; generated by the previous objectives.

In this mutual relationship, the productivity gain leads to a reduced management effort from buyer's side, since the active involvement, as well as the passive involvement can be reduced. This again leads to the possibility to allocate the resources required for the management and/or a higher efficiency of this particular supplier relationship, since with less input a higher output can be realized. On the other side, the productivity increase has a positive impact on the supplier as well. Since within this improvement process the company culture regarding quality, commitment and problems are improved, the whole supplier organization will profit from it with an increase of efficiency and reliability. This leads directly to less waste and a release of capacity for other orders or a bigger order volume. All these factors have direct impact on the (short-term) profit gained from an order.

The growth objective is meant to be a long-term strategy benefiting from the improvements, but there is also short-term impact present here, because aspects from the productivity strategy are directly linked to the profit/the savings achieved. For the buyer this means that his strategy to source low cost from a Chinese supplier begins to have impact on the savings, leading to a better competitiveness. The supplier, who has increased gains now, is motivated as he realizes the impact of improvement. Using the profit for further improvements, he can execute continuous improvement actions, which – besides of the evident advantages – lead to a better standing in the market not only locally, but also internationally.

6.2.3 Strategy map for SI to meet minimum requirements

In order to improve the supplier's capabilities three major strategic objectives have to be followed: (1) to reduce the deficiencies in the supplier's business functions, which were found in the audit; (2) to undertake actions to reduce the risks occurring for the buyer and the supplier, and (3) after the first order, to implement initiatives to improve the processes, which lead to the product dissatisfaction. Therefore in the scope of this work a Strategy Map was developed (as basis for a BSC), which follows the strategy: "Close the audit-found deficits, the risks connected to this sourcing activity and improve the product, in order to achieve besides of enhanced capabilities a win-win partnership, with increased profit, market share and possibilities for the supplier." (see Figure 6.4) This strategic objective is subordinated to the buyer supplier relationship improvement, since it is a part of it.

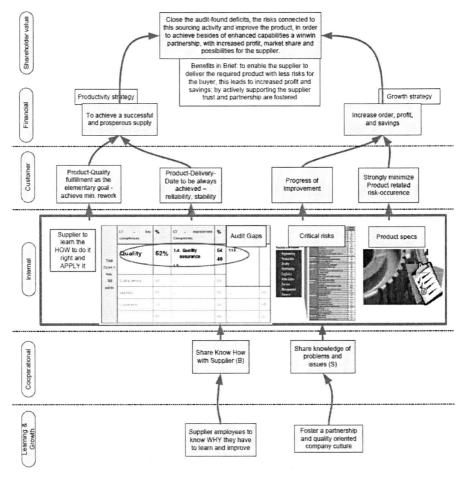

Figure 6.4 Template Strategy Map for a holistic capability improvement

The audit strategy map gives an overview over the required objectives to accomplish in order to support the improvement of capabilities. These capabilities to improve are based on the findings in the audit, the risk assessment and on the dissatisfying product. They are referred to as improvement components (see chapter 6.3.2.1). The consideration of the five perspectives of the buyer supplier relationship brings the advantage to recognize the steps and the needs leading to the improvement strategy, which makes the shareholder value rise. Further, the dependencies of the improvement objectives are visualized and connected to the activities within the resulting BSC.

a) Learning and Growth perspective

As in the relationship improvement related strategy map the understanding is essential for the supplier improvement BSC as well. If the supplier agrees on improvement only in order to get the contract, without motivation and self commitment, no success can be expected. The supplier has to see an advantage that is worth the effort. Depending on the supplier's strategy and his company culture the WHY of learning and improvement can differ. The right approach from buyer's side towards the executives is essential, in order to convince them of the benefits.

This perspective also includes the cultivation of the company culture and the quality thinking, with the aim to increase the sharing of information (required for problem solving) or to assure lastingness (process-oriented improvement, cp. 3.1.4). As it is culture, this is a long-term objective. The quality orientation has to be based on learning, understanding, experience and motivation. Active and personal involvement may be the best way to foster this strategic objective. In contrast to the latter strategic objective presented, the buyer is in this case not only active towards the supplier, but also his own employees. It is required that the procurement's employees' understanding of partnership is facilitated; it has to be clear, why it is required to put so much effort into a supplier company and relationship.

b) Cooperation perspective

Since the employees are aware of the benefits of improvement now, but may lack know-how in order to achieve the goals, the buyer can provide information to them. The initiatives to undertake against risks and deficits are jointly determined and have to be executed by the supplier's employees. The buyer's improvement team can await results, stay by side and/ or consult them in the case of emerging questions and issues and/ or directly participate.

The buyer's improvement team applies these improvement activities soon after beginning to overview the problems and possible solutions, so that it should take advantage of its existing knowledge and support the supplier strongly. But, in order to improve, the problems need to be shared by the supplier's employees. Therefore, the creation of trust is important. However, no company likes to share information on problems, since the information could cause damage, if not treated confidentially. So, it might be necessary to foster this process of information sharing. For example it can be stressed and explained, why reporting of problems is rather an achievement (instead of "losing the face") and an unsatisfactory supply results in a disadvantage. Incentives could help to facilitate this.

c) Internal processes perspective

This internal processes perspective has the strategic objective to decrease the critical deficiencies of the supplier's business processes found in the audit, risk assessment and in the supplied product. From these three characteristics the improvement components can be derived (see chapter 6.3.2.1). Within the BSC the critical issues can be ranked higher, initiatives planned and undertaken, and then the improvement components monitored upon improvement progress. By executing this improvement undertaking, the supplier's employees have to be strongly involved, in order to avoid repetition of issues. The supplier has to understand the causes and the ways of avoiding them. The buyer's improvement team can give active support with these issues.

d) Customer perspective

The execution of initiatives in order to improve the supplier's capabilities has impact on both supplier and buyer. The supplier can achieve higher efficiencies and lower risks, which go hand in hand with many further advantages (less waste generates higher profit, capacity increase, better standing in the market etc.). However, the strategic aim followed by the improvement is to deliver higher value to the customer.

Fulfilling the product quality has the advantage that there is fewer rework. The reduction of rework is directly connected to higher profit for the supplier, since rework is "profitless" and requires material, capacity and time. Therefore, this can be seen as a motivating objective. For the buyer this has the obvious advantage that he attains the ordered products but also the productivity of the sales is increased ("more value/savings for less effort/supplier management"). Furthermore, since the rework issue costs supplier management effort from buyer's side due to "order repetition" and discussion, it can result in frustration for both buyer and supplier, thus damaging the relationship and wasting both companies' time and capacity.

Another major characteristic of a successful supply is the meeting of the delivery time. It means for the buyer that he can benefit from the supplied product. If the supply is delayed it may be required to cancel the order or reorder at another supplier. This means increased management and product costs for the buyer. For the supplier this leads to no profit from the work invested. The highest risk for the buyer is to pay penalties (e.g. towards the final customer), if the delay of the product can't be compensated and the production has to be stopped. To enable the buyer to plan, stability has to be reached, which at least allows predictability (regarding delivery and quality).

The progress of improvement is a key element to follow with the whole strategy. "There is always room for improvement" one of the interviewees stated. The progress of improvement means that audit gaps are being closed, risks diminished and the products increasingly meet requirements. Each of the improved business processes or business elements leads to higher value of the relationship, differentiating "this" relationship from the other ones in China: "The best supporting buyer and the best improving supplier". This improvement has to be monitored and fostered. If there is progress, both supplier and buyer can benefit, by growing their businesses.

The minimization of product related risk is, as the attainment of quality and delivery, one of the main objectives for the buyer, because every risk decreases the savings due to its certain monetary value (cp. chapter 3.1.3). Thus, controlling processes to reduce relevant risks have to be established. This aim has to be followed as soon as possible after the cooperation was started.

e) Financial perspective

Since the attainment of a long term partnership is the highest aim of the buyer supplier relationship and for the improvement, it has to be fostered to enable synergies and high efficiency and to give security (productivity strategy). When supporting the growth of the buyer supplier relationship, the results can be a rising variety of products and order volumes, due to good capabilities and reduced risks, and growing shareholder value, since the profit and savings both are increased as well.

6.3 Improvement Balanced Scorecard

The Improvement Balanced Scorecard is derived from the improvement strategy maps described above. The BSC allows tracking the progress of the state to the given targets, and thereby the state to the strategic objectives. It visualizes the measures with the performance target set and gives an overview over the initiatives, which represent the actions to undertake to reach for the targets.

Further the Balanced Scorecard gives the basis for the project-plan for improvement, since it includes in its part "action plan" the owner (the responsible person for the initiative) and the budget, which is approved. In this work the BSC is designed in the shape recommended by Kaplan and Norton (/Kap-04/), since it gives a good overview and includes the main required parts. The strategy map was divided into strategic themes (A,B,C,D) to create better overview ability.

Objectives, Measures, Targets and Initiatives

The Balanced Scorecard has the great advantage of being flexible regarding its measures. To every strategic objective certain measures have to be found in order to monitor the progress of improvement. As Creelman and Makhijani (/Cre-05/) oppose to have more than 2 measures per strategic objective included. The idea is, to consider only the "critical few", which really are required to assess the progress towards the objective. In the designed Relationship Balanced Scorecard, the number is for many strategic objectives higher in order to illustrate, but has to be decreased for application, according to the emerging constraints and suitability for the given relationship.

There also needs to be a balance between the measures included – the one between the so called "leading and lagging" measures. The lagging ones are the classical key performance indicators: they measure past performance and do not provide information on what will happen in the future. The leading indicators give "information about what is happening that will impact performance tomorrow" (/Cre-05/). In some cases, the measure can have both leading and lagging characteristics. An example from the relationship BSC: the measure "delayed delivery" is a typical lagging indicator; in contrast, the measure "capabilities/percentage of audit gap" will have impact on the quality and delivery tomorrow. This represents, according to the deficits of former approaches, one of the advantages of this concept.

The measures can be chosen flexibly, so they can have a monetary value, contain ratios or different values (x, order, readiness, period etc.) and it is strongly recommended to connect them to a timeframe or period. The targets have to express, in which direction the strategic objective has to go. They should be stretching in nature, so that they are motivating. However, if they are not achievable the opposite case may occur. One of the big difficulties between buyer and supplier may emerge when the buyer has to explain to the supplier that the targets to reach are not a controlling or "punishing" mechanism, but a tool for continuous improvement (/Cre-05/). A further problem may be that the measures or the measuring mechanisms are not available yet, because they differ strongly from the former ones; this increases the difficulty of implementation and of finding meaningful measures.

The intangible assets have to be measured as well, for this reason Kaplan and Norton (/Kap-04/) recommend to measure the readiness: The "readiness is the extent to which an intangible asset is aligned with the strategy". The intangible assets have to be managed also, so that the readiness gets improved. In order to do that, each asset has to have a readiness defined, which can be measured and managed.

Eventually, after a period (e.g. weekly, monthly, or quarterly) of BSC application the corresponding targets are compared with the status. This check gives feedback on whether the improvement initiative has positive impact, how big this impact is, and if the results are not satisfying, why latter weren't reached. In latter case, a stronger involvement may be realized in the future, or the initiative changed, to reach the given target. Forker states (/For-99/) that although there may be a well designed supplier improvement plan, it is still inevitable that it is well communicated and fully understood by the supplier. Misunderstandings about the objective aimed for decrease its effectiveness strongly. There have to be continual checks on the mutual agreement resulting in higher productivity, since the actions are undertaken into the right direction.

Similarly to the risk approaches presented by Fleischer or Wildemann (cp. 3.1.3) the initiatives planned have to be evaluated upon their impact and effectiveness, and whether the costs they save compensate the costs they produce. Hence, the initiative has to be assessed on its dependencies to other initiatives first, so that it has no negative impact on other processes; and if it does, which one has to be prioritized, and whether it can be excluded, has to be further analyzed. The remaining initiative needs evaluation on required budget from both buyer and supplier, and whether it is reasonable for the case at hand. Often there are only estimations for the calculation available, unless an in deep cost analysis was conducted. In the case of monetary assessed risks (Fleischer /Fle-06/ cp. 3.1.3) the estimation is eased by having a monetary value, which changes by reducing the probability of occurrence or the severity, or rising the probability of detection. However, also Fleischer states that the risk assessment is difficult after the sharing measures were decided, because there are correlations between the single risks.

6.3.1 Buyer Supplier Relationship BSC

Founded on the in chapter 6.2.2 presented Strategy Map for buyer supplier relationship Improvement a Balanced Scorecard was designed. Like the strategy map it has five perspectives and strives to improve both companies' relationship. This intangible connection between two companies is considered as an asset or an entity, which requires improvement in order to achieve a better result for both companies.

Further, the BSC is based on the findings from desktop research and the interviews and strives for the fulfillment of the IC buyer's requirements (a satisfying supply and supplier relationship) and the Chinese supplier's aims (increased profit, efficient processes, and fulfillment of the buyer's requirements). In this BSC, the customer perspective is represented by the buyer, the internal processes perspective by the supplier, and the relationship specific issues are considered in the cooperation perspective.

The according strategy map was divided into four strategic themes (A,B,C,D) to increase overview and the traceability, but the four resulting scorecards have the same level and have to be considered as one BSC (see the whole BSC in chapter B Annex). Therefore, in single cases the measures and objectives may overlap. Further, the BSC presented in the following shows initiatives, which were created for illustrative reasons under the consideration of the described findings (interviews, desktop research) with alignment to the strategic objectives. However, as every problem has to be approached by an individual solution, the initiatives are not to be considered fixed. From its nature, the whole BSC presented underlies certain flexibility. Nevertheless, the cause and effects in the strategy map as the objectives and the measures have a reasoning, which is described in the following.

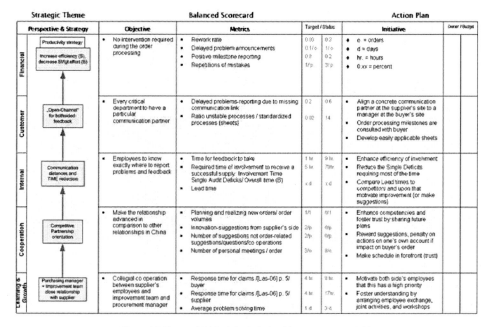

Figure 6.5 Theme-A-BSC of the Relationship Improvement BSC

6.3.1.1 Theme A

In the Learning & Growth perspective of this theme the intangible asset "employees" are part of the improvement. They are the basis of the relationship. The triangle set up from purchasing manager, improvement team and the supplier's employees (including the executive level) is responsible for a functioning & improving relationship. Therefore a collegial cooperation is required. The measures chosen are the response time for claims (on both sides) and the average problem solving time. They can be enhanced by joint activities of key responsibilities for a higher familiarity among each other. For the not executive level employees bonus programs are recommended, so that commitment can be rewarded.

The well connected employees are responsible for driving the competitive relationship, which naturally helps on the Chinese market (also because of the Guanxi). By improving the relationship, a competitive partnership can be attained, which includes mutual planning and both sided support regarding issues. The supplier has to be convinced of the benefit he can attain by undertaking the needed effort. So planning of future orders and profit can be trust and motivation creating. Rewards to increase the direct profit can be offered. A schedule regarding the improvement activities has to be developed and steadily monitored. The schedule fosters trust, as both sides agree on it in forefront.

Partnership oriented employees have easier communication of issues. However, this also has to be supported by the structure, where a single information line with clear responsibilities must exist. Measure for this can be the feedback time as basic measure. The required involvement time of the buyer to attain a successful supply shows the communicability/understanding and the maturity of the supplier. Lead time can be taken into consideration if it is impacted by waiting times due to unclearness or misunderstandings. In order to decrease the time of involvement, its efficiency needs to be increased, better planning and structure. The reduction of certain critical deficits and the comparison of the lead times to competitors for motivation are the suggested approaches to execute.

This "open-channel" represents the buyer's wish to be able to always get/give feedback to the supplier. So it is part of supplier management improvement. It gives also a certain reliability increase due the enabled easy check on the processing status. The measurement of the "delayed problem reporting" (earlier reporting leads to earlier solution) can be avoided by restructuring the responsibilities. Furthermore, standardized and easy applicable formalized feedback is suggested. Establishing positive reporting milestones in the production process can increase motivation and show the problem drivers.

Eventually, when an order requires minimal intervention and management effort, one of the main objectives of the buyer is reached. The supplier attained stable processes, an increased efficiency and capacity, and thus more orders. The objective increased profit is accomplished. This can be measured by rework rate, delayed problem announcements, and the fulfillment of nearly all "positive milestones". The repetition of mistakes shows the maturity of the supplier to adapt to the lessons learnt.

6.3.1.2 Theme B

The understanding of the WHY emerged to be one of the most crucial factors for improvement. Since the relationship is based on both companies also both of them have to support its improvement. The buyer is the driving force of improvement since he has the know how and demands the improvement in order to see his requirements met. This is possible only if the supplier is fully convinced of this. To measure the degree of the readiness of alignment with the mutual strategy (as required cp. /Kap-04/) the number of active involvements in case of occurring problems is chosen. There occurs a conflict with the aim to increase the reporting of problems. It has to be chosen, which of this objectives has to be prioritized. The other one has to be optimized (/Las-06/). The readiness of the supplier's employees' to support the improvement process has also to be checked. To achieve that, the direct loss through waste (e.g. rework, inefficiency, order cancellation etc.) has to be visualized and also a long term orientation fostered. Incentives can be helpful for the non-executive level employees. Mutual strategy fosters the required win-win situation.

The mutually beneficial activities can be measured by expressing direct benefits for both sides. So, here the amount of strategic co-operations, the time an order takes to be processed (from beginning to decision), or the height of bonuses given upon improved quality or delivery rate can be used for measurement. To achieve the targets, trust has to be fostered, so strategic co-operations have to be implemented (e.g. the material quality may be low, so the procurement could be a strategic cooperation option). A bonus pool has to be created and increased upon positive effect.

The operational monitoring has the aim to uncover the supplier's processes, which are lacking efficiency and quality, having impact on the product/supply characteristics. However, these are not directly connected to the improvement of capabilities or the supplier audit. They are long term oriented and serve the supplier and buyer to overview the bottlenecks for deep insight. The found inefficiencies have to be decreased, as well as the wasted time (no value adding). In order to assure proper quality is delivered, the efficiency of quality gates has to be increased (x found defects/x not found defects – found by buyer). As illustrative approaches can be mentioned, cost analysis, TQM education and application, the standardization of processes and the assignment of responsibilities to each of the processes needing improvement.

For the buyer it is important to be able to rely on the supplier's performance. Besides of the quality and delivery, he has to predict the future supply's characteristics to be able to plan. Even if the supply is not meeting the requirements fully, a stable quality attainment may be better than a volatile one. Many problems are brought in by the 2nd and 3rd tier suppliers. Therefore attention has to be paid to the problems in the supplier's procurement. Both the development of delayed delivery and the rework rate (triggered by buyer or supplier) give information on the stability of the supplier's processes (similarly to the found defects in the above paragraph). Further, latter data gives information on the supplier's maturity to control his own performance in quality. As initiatives, the key-sub supplier's sites can be approached in order to achieve (in cooperation with the supplier) improvement. Further, the supplier's receipt control can be improved, or last, active involvement can be increased to participate in the critical processes helping to fulfill the order.

With a stable quality and delivery the risks of sudden critical problems are minimized, thereby reducing the management effort (planning gets more precise). This leads to increased productivity gains, which are also supported by the supplier's enhanced processes and the bonuses for increased performance. Interesting may be the costs invested in comparison to the order costs: they may stay high in the beginning of the relationship, but decrease over the longer term. The supplier can measure his benefit from his input by observing the development of the profit to turnover ratio.

6.3.1.3　Theme C

As explained before, the understanding is indispensable. The design of a competency profile in the scope of the readiness report (cp. 6.3) is recommended. This competency profile can be worked out for both buyer and supplier. This has, besides of increased trust, the effect that an understanding of the required competencies can be developed. The buyer has to increase his competency regarding the supplier consulting and educate the suppliers personnel regarding the lacking capabilities; consultancy by the means of suggestions. The supplier, in contrast, has to allow and appreciate suggestions, not taking it as foreign takeover, and support the buyer's undertakings.

A win-win situation requires that changes and corrective actions have to be decided jointly, since it can have impact on both companies. Therefore, detrimental actions have to be decreased to zero by the means of a standard list for changes (as a "good improvements" list, in order to motivate the supplier to improve; a regularly review is suggested). More severe changes have always to be consulted with the according communication partner. Further, giving bonuses increases the profit for the supplier, when the buyer has increased benefit from better performance. The measure "monetary amount given" gives information on the satisfaction level.

In order to satisfy the buyer's requirements the supplier has to improve certain capabilities in the forefront. So a short term improvement is required, closing the main gaps and major risks to assure a successful supply. The status of this goal can be measured by the specific improvements decided; being not in time according the time schedule is a current indicator showing that immediate action is required. The decrease of risk and rework rate, as the increase of capabilities, show the improvement also. In order to drive the performance in the case of "behind schedule" an increase of active involvement (or of its efficiency) is suggested, to accelerate the supplier's advance. In order to avoid the problem of rework and risk (triggered by buyer), quality checkpoints giving positive feedback can be established. Further, to avoid the risk of dissatisfying supply, the order can be postponed to take down the pressure.

The strategy the buyer follows with procurement in China is to attain competitive products. These competitive products ideally fulfill the same requirements like in an Industrialized Country at the price level of China. To follow this objective, the ratio quality rate and the price rate (in comparison to the German one) to the last order has to be improved. Quality complaints itself have to be reduced, and the delivery reliability increased. In order to do that, the differences between IC and Chinese suppliers have to be steadily watched. The production process planning can be supported by the buyer, since he often has the necessary knowledge. However, the supplier has to fulfill decided plans. At the time of decreasing involvement, the price has to decrease as well. The benefits have to be shared fairly.

In the end, the growth strategy is supported by increased savings and profit. To measure the success the savings in comparison to the last order can be viewed. The supplier can follow the development of his profit/turnover ratio compared to last orders.

6.3.1.4 Theme D

By assuring knowledge to be lasting, the buyer can save resources and decrease risk. In China frequently changing employees make this difficult. So the key staff retention rate has to be focused. According to (/Gro-06/) the key responsibilities in China have biggest interest in their possibilities of career development, their yearly raise of salary and a satisfying company culture. Further bonuses for improvement announcements can be possible motivating incentives. Therefore, the HR programs of the supplier can be supported by the buyer (e.g. as part of the paid incentives or as constraint to get a bigger order). An improvement log might have the advantage to enable a follow up to understand the improvement process for a new employee. Standard procedures have to be known by at least two supplier's employees to avoid a high dependence on single employees.

The relationship has to become a long term partnership, as it is the wish of the buyer, and regularly the supplier as well. In order to support this aim, the employees of both companies have to create a "friendship" between them, as it is common in China. Therefore the supplier's and the buyer's trust have to be increased by "fair" contracts (supportive, win-win etc.), and e.g. cultural activities involving the key responsibilities. Also the involvement and training of supplier's employees can count to the joint investments, which increase the mutual trust and tighten the relationship. The degree of trust has to be measured in the readiness report, as it is a basic element of a partnership.

In the internal perspectives of this theme, the consideration of risks is focused. Since the employees increase their know-how and bind it, and the inter-organizational relationships are growing, a holistic risk assessment has to be emphasized in order to secure the both companies' monetary success. Risk Assessment tools could be established in both companies, in order to avoid problems to occur. An important indicator is also the not reported risk, which is recognized at supplier's site, but not reported. Latter one can be avoided and improved by gathering feedback from the supplier's employees responsible for the production process, with following support. Unmanaged risks can occur from buyer's side also, if he knows about an issue, but does not consider it serious enough. In every case, the cause for a not detected risk has to be found and initiatives to avoid repetition implemented.

The best value for the IC buyer is attained when high reliability meets low cost on every level. A stretching objective is, when the Chinese supplier is being compared to a realistic performance of an IC, e.g. German, supplier. So the overall performance is measured and compared with the "German supplier" in order to find the gap. The same procedure can be used to see the development of the price. So, the price is compared to the average of Chinese suppliers. In order to attain an in depth overview, a strong involvement is required and a cost analysis implemented.

Latter of course can be difficult, since the supplier's are afraid of getting too transparent. However, this difficulty can be faced already with other issues within the BSC. The critical departments can be assessed more often and supervised to attain given targets (e.g. performance, or improvement components).

In the end the supplier has the advantage of getting bonuses due to the achieved improvements, and the buyer attained a satisfying supply, worth the bonuses. It would be a waste of effort if the buyer would not source in the future from the supplier, and since he is already improved, the risks are lower. As a consequence, increased orders probably bring higher margins for the supplier and the required product for the buyer.

6.3.2 "Audit-BSC" to Boost Supplier's Capabilities

The Audit Balanced Scorecard is part of the relationship improvement process and thus part of the buyer supplier relationship improvement BSC (see Annex). It has the aim to improve the supplier in an efficient way so that he can supply parts reliably, fulfilling the buyer's requirements as soon as possible. As it considers the occurring risks, the supplier's deficient capabilities and the product itself, it gives a proper basis for the improvement of the buyer supplier relationship.

The risks emerging from a Chinese supplier can be diversified in two categories: an environmental and a product-related category. In the scope of this work, and especially for the Audit BSC, only the product related risks are considered (the environmental ones could be included into the overall BSC to approach them on a strategic basis). Product related risks mean all the issues occurring with a certain probability, which can cause financial damage by having negative impact on the supply of a satisfying product.

Deficient processes are identified in the supplier assessment (as described in chapter 3.1.2). The assessment tool presented by Wagner (/Wag-06/) delivers an overview over present deficits. The most critical ones have to be identified, examined upon possible connections to the critical risks and the impact on the resulting product have to be analyzed. These critical issues (improvement components) have to be included into the improvement plan, according to their impact, urgency and dependencies to other objectives or improvement components. After the first order the buying organization identifies the product-deficits and discusses it with the supplier. From the overall data collected, the processes that caused the problem have to be identified and improved with an according priority, since they represent a potential risk.

From these three characteristics (product related risks, audit results and product) the improvement components are found. Taking the most critical ones from each and recognizing their connections and dependencies enables the derivation of the most urgent improvement components (further description in chapter 6.3.2.1).

The Audit Scorecard has the aim to boost the supplier's capabilities up to a minimum level to make a supply process possible. In the beginning, naturally, the highest risks and deficits in the supplier's business structure have to be emphasized. However, as it includes all the critical elements showing deficits it can be used to monitor continuously the improvement progress during the regular buyer supplier relationship. Further, it can be used for advance notice so that early intervention is possible.

Since cost savings have to be achieved by the sourcing in China, the expenses for the supplier improvement have to stay within a certain limit. Therefore the budget calculation of the initiatives is reasonable. The calculated required budget can then be compared to the monetary value of the risk minimized and then the initiative suggested evaluated upon reasonability.

However, since the improvement should be basis for a long term relationship, the price for the product (including the expenses for improvement) has not to be the primary measure.

6.3.2.1 Improvement Components

Improvement components[2] are the business processes and elements that need improvement, since they are responsible for certain capabilities. They can result from the supplier assessment (if lacking fulfillment of requirements), from the risk assessment (if they were found to be the root cause of a risk), or from the dissatisfying supplied product (if they were found to be the reason for the dissatisfying characteristic).

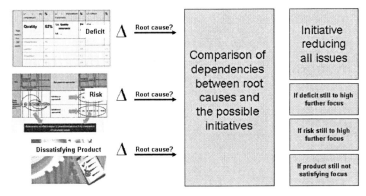

Figure 6.6 Improvement components from Assessments and product specs

In order to improve the deficits, reduce the risk, attain wished product, and increase the capabilities, the buyer has to think of the root causes in order to avoid them. Once, the root causes are identified, they can be aligned and analyzed upon dependencies and similarities. The similar problems can often be treated at the same time. If there are not similarities and dependencies, the issues require individual initiatives. Further, it is required to know, whether possible initiatives to avoid them, do not work against each other, or let occur another risk. In the following a short illustration is given.

---

[2] Improvement components could be referred to as development components as well, since "supplier development" may mean the improvement respectively the increase of capabilities (cp. /Wag-06/).

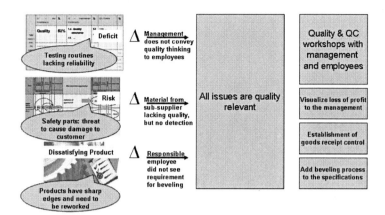

Figure 6.7 Illustration of finding improvement components

This example is considering the supply of safety parts from the supplier that have quality issues. The audit identified a problem in the category "Quality", the "testing routines lack reliability", e.g. because of a not standardized proceeding. However, the cause for this issue can be the employee in the operating process, but the root cause may be the management, which does not provide the basic elements for a standardized proceeding (e.g. a checklist). Furthermore, one of the critical identified risks is the following: since the material received from the sub supplier may be low quality, there is a threat to the safety of the final customer, which is not acceptable for the buyer. The root cause for this issue would be the sub supplier. However, since the influence on latter one may require too high effort, the lacking of quality control in the goods-receipt may be considered as root cause, which can be avoided by certain risk sharing measures. And further, after the first supply, it was recognized that there are sharp edges, making rework necessary. This would be a product characteristic, which was not discussed in the forefront maybe, but is required to be considered. The cause here may be an employee in processing, who just did not see the necessity of beveling the edge.

The dependency between the issues is "Quality Commitment". This commitment could be considered as improvement component. As initiative against this problem Quality and Quality Control workshops could be organized, for management and production employees and also goods receive employees. This may improve the understanding of quality and solve some elementary problems. Alternatively, in order to make the improvements working on the short term, the root causes have to be avoided immediately. Thus, these root causes can be called improvement components as well. The single initiatives for the single capabilities have to attend the essential problems. Both the overall initiative of "quality thinking support" and the initiatives to improve the processes responsible for the company culture may be executed according to Hartley and Jones simultaneously (/Har-97/) (cp. chapter 3.1.4).

Eventually, these improvement components can be aligned to a Balanced Scorecard, to measure the progress of improvement. Naturally, this needs to be done carefully, since every BSC and every measure are cause for measurement and monitoring, so that too many of them would rather make the problem worse than solve it. However, an overview can be given in order to focus the most critical issues. The advantage of the BSC approach is that the measures can be chosen flexibly, since it has no restrictions (it has to be kept in mind that it has to be measurable and this measurement repeatable, and preferably the measures both lagging and leading). Laschke (/Las-06/ p. 2) states, that the, integrated measures do not have to be aggregateable into the superior BSC. The connecting element is a structure of objectives, which is part of the overall objective.

6.3.2.2 Description of the Audit BSC

The Audit strategy map was not divided into themes as the relationship improvement strategy map, since it has fewer themes in the first case. Second the aim of it is to "boost the supplier's capabilities" to ensure the supply. If considering each possible critical process, this Balanced Scorecard would be overloaded. Anyway, since each supplier needs other processes to focus on (depending on the results, products) this would not make sense. Therefore, only the major required objectives were chosen to be included, to support the improvement (Audit BSC see Annex).

The supplier improvement depends on the participation of the supplier's executive employees, so they need to be convinced of it. In order to enable the buyer to consult them and make suggestions on the possible solutions, the employees have to be ready to report issues and problems. However, one of the problems of the Chinese employees is that they don't want to "lose the face" and thus would not report any problem. So, the supplier's employees have to know WHY it is required to report, why to learn and why to improve processes lacking efficiency. They also have to have a certain way of reporting, which eases it. For this, the measure ratio of employees to report problems to the ones who do not report problems is taken. It may be supported with a method where employees can anonymously write down issues in the processes and get an incentive for that. Another measure may be the bonuses paid for suggestions made and problems solved. The bonus pool has to have a certain amount and be increased from time to time to motivate the employees.

In the cooperation perspective the sharing of knowledge is emphasized. On the one side it is the supplier's employees who have to report problems; on the other side the buyer mustn't be reluctant to share the knowledge, but to give suggestions without dictating. Here, the measure number of suggestions from buyer's side is taken; the ratio of realized suggestions to the made suggestions gives information on the supplier's willingness to implement them. A possible help to increase these factors is the reasoning approach, which has to be adapted to the supplier's strategy (e.g. short term profit) or the involvement of a cross-functional team that is responsible for fast feedback with fitting solutions on issues.

As the main part of the Audit Balanced Scorecard the improvement of the supplier's processes has to be focused. As presented in the chapter improvement components this improvement includes product characteristics, risks and the audit results. The supplier now has consultancy from buyer's side. However, he has to learn the HOW to create improvements and convert this knowledge into action. The single most critical improvement components are hereby the measures to monitor the progress of improvement. Another indicator chosen is the not executed improvements at due date. These not executed improvements may have a reason. It may be that the supplier is not committed enough, or that he didn't get enough support. The causes have to be found, and, in every case, the solutions have to be found and applied. In the case that there is too little improvement, the according initiative has to be reconsidered.

With the improvement of the missing capabilities and processes the buyer's minimum requirements have to be met. Therefore, concurrent monitoring is required to assure the achievement of a stable supply fulfilling the demanded quality and delivery. In order to attain this strategic objective reliably, it is suggested to follow the quality and delivery problems already during the processing. Here the problem of interdependency occurs again. On the one hand, every issue requires reporting; on the other hand, the amount of issues has to decrease over time. As possible approach an increased amount of quality feedback milestones could be established. If the product/the process does fulfill given requirements it is reported to the responsibility in order to tackle this issue. So the number of reporting should be high. However, if complaints occur from the buyer's side, it is already too late to avoid a problem in time. Then an analysis can show which process was responsible. Repetition of problems is highly dissatisfying, new problems should be decreased. In the beginning of course, the amount of occurring new problems is high, since they have to be found and solved first. In order to drive these measures, the initiatives have to optimize feedback. Already mentioned was the approach with the feedback gates. Further, lastingness can be approached by standardization and zero-defects approaches. Eventually increased incentives and anonymity can be facilitating.

With this Balanced Scorecard the objective to attain a non-risky (less risky) fulfillment of supply was followed. The decrease of risks for both supplier and buyer leads directly to increased savings and profit. So the risk decrease amount /percent per period (buyer) can be measured. The success can also be measured by the deliveries in time/not in time and the amount of complaints causing rework in comparison to the total order volume, which is directly connected to both parties savings and profit as well (for the supplier no bonuses and rework is "loss of money", buyer has twice the management effort).

6.4 Organizational integration of the BSC

The practical implementation of the Balanced Scorecard approach is a further question. However, it should not be discussed in detail in the scope of this work. The BSC is a method, which allows individual adaptation flexible to the situation between the buyer and the supplier. It would be an advantage if the buyer, as introducing party, would already have experience with application of the BSC.

As mentioned before, the implementation of the Balanced Scorecard is in this case in the hands of the buyer's procurement manager (the involved improvement team) and the supplier's executives, who are responsible for the implementation of the objectives and initiatives in their company. The buyer is the customer who transfers his direct requirements to the supplier, and additionally, the know-how that is required to attain these requirements. The supplier is responsible for the processes that are required in order to supply and their improvement. Latter one may be supported by the buyer's improvement team. Therefore, both supplier and buyer have to cooperate to apply this method. By doing so, they already fulfill one of the main prerequisites for the BSC, the partnership orientation. Therefore, it is a further requirement that the buyer and the supplier in this relationship work on an equal level of market power.

The responsibilities for the single initiatives referring to certain objectives have to be found dependent on the issue. The scorecard should include a balanced number of supplier's and buyer's objectives and initiatives owners. If it is not equal, the supplier should have a higher number of owners, since the changes are applied at the supplier's site. The buyer may have the interest to control whether the data provided is correct. In the interviews conducted it was stated that data may be false, not because of lacking trust, but given by the fact that often the know how to attain properly measured data is not available. The buyer supervision of the measurement, however, needs a careful approach to avoid supplier's loss of trust. Furthermore, the buyer has to emphasize an in depth instruction of how the BSC is to be applied (for possible implementation problems see next chapter).

Further, the execution on a software basis is recommended in order to increase efficiency. The software is not of essential interest, whereas MS Excel probably may be available at the supplier's site. Important is the consequent orientation (/Las-06/) of the different departments and levels to follow one strategy. In consideration to the supplier's other customers, the supplier's application of the BSC may be enlarged to succeed with them. This may support the success of the approach eminently, since the effort to undertake wouldn't burden only one relationship. However, to do so, the supplier would have to implement an own "major Balanced Scorecard", which would include the goals to achieve with the relationship Balanced Scorecards of all relationships. The single BSCs have to improve the relationship between buyer and supplier. Hence, it can be applied only for single relationships. For the buyer the situation is similar. Every relationship BSC counts for one relationship only, but he can have a higher ranked BSC, which coordinates the objectives of the relationship BSCs.

7 Discussion

In the chapters "Basics", "State of the Art in Research" and in "Today's issues of the Industry's supplier development in China" discussion shows that the supplier improvement in China is a required approach for an Industrialized Country buyer (mechanical engineering investment goods), in order to attain the required quality, delivery reliability at low risk and cost from the supplier. Therefore an improvement approach based on the Balanced Scorecard was designed, striving for the fulfillment of the needs and the improvement of a buyer supplier relationship in China. Further, it seeks the enhancement of supplier improvement, and at the same time for the avoidance of emerging barriers. In the following, this approach is analyzed upon the advantages and the possible limitations for the implementation in buyer supplier relationships respectively the both companies. In this work, the emphasis lies on mechanical engineering companies, sourcing low volumes with high specialization. For the given companies supplier development in China is, in contrast to the home market, rather strategic: it is connected to a high effort and risk on the long term and there are relatively few suppliers, which have the required qualification. Therefore, the potential suppliers have to be improved according to the specific requirements from buyer's side. In order to make the improvement successful and lasting the Chinese supplier's wishes necessitate consideration.

The essential improvement characteristics underlie a pattern, which does not differ strongly from the one in Industrialized Countries, e.g. win-win situation, necessity of good communication, or the need for commitment from both sides. But, at the case at hand, the business relations are of intercultural nature, the suppliers have differing strategies, other company culture and also other viewpoints on product requirements. Thus, the approach conducted within this work has to be evaluated upon the consideration and fulfillment of the fundamental and the special requirements in China, and whether it is satisfying the desire for a relationship improvement tool. The approach with the Balanced Scorecard has the advantage that it enables to include the different aspects of a relationship that need to be considered and improved. So, in addition to the four perspectives of an organization, the fifth perspective "cooperation" contains the elements that are essential to tie the two companies. The presented buyer supplier relationship improvement process has the advantage that it fosters trust and understanding by visualization and transparency. So, the strategic objectives to follow in order to reach the major strategy of the "entity" buyer supplier relationship in China are shown. The entity has to be improved in order to grow and become stronger, leading to benefits for both companies. These two companies are the groundwork for the relationship; their employees, processes and strategies drive the relationship. Therefore, these factors are to be aligned and coordinated, as the entity has the eventual strategic objective, to become a partnership – which is regularly the highest aim in a relationship.

However, there are limitations of the presented approach. The Balanced Scorecard is originally a tool to enhance the strategic orientation of a company, including all parts of the company. Here, the BSC strives for the improvement of all parts of a single relationship, which is developing between buyer's procurement and supplier's employees with the interactions taking place. So, it is only a part of each company, which is involved into this relationship. Every part has to orient itself to the own company's strategy and can't be completely dedicated to the strategy of the relationship-BSC. But, it is imaginable that companies decide to implement latter BSC into their overall strategy and, thus, enable the implementation of relationship BSCs for all relationships. However, this would mean a high effort to undertake, and for the Chinese supplier, who is not "used" applying strategic methods, this may represent a big barrier. For the buyer it is improbable to implement the improvement initiative "introduce a BSC system at the supplier's site". Further can be said that already the implementation with one company represents for the supplier a big effort, since he has to introduce new performance indicators, a new strategy and change the thinking of his employees (latter one can possibly be the biggest barrier). Another situation would emerge if both companies already use the BSC as strategic management tool: on the one hand this may ease the situation, since both companies have experience with the BSC; on the other hand it has the issue, that the companies' BSCs probably would not have the cooperation perspective – for this, translations to the superior Scorecards would have to be developed.

Another characteristic of the BSC approach is that it requires full commitment. The strategy map fosters the understanding of the aims, but the commitment of the supplier has to develop by itself and in forefront of application; the supplier has to support it fully, in order to begin. This may emerge to be difficult according to the Chinese supplier culture. However, it could be facilitated prioritizing few objectives and patient implementation. Therefore, the Audit BSC strives for an implementation with few strategic and rather operational objectives to accelerate the process. Further, it is mentioned that the BSC has to foster the trust and the communication. The communicability of issues is enhanced, since both companies have the same template and are geared to it. Though, in two companies, foreign to each other, a disagreement on certain topics is very probable. Therefore, the measures, strategic objectives and the targets have to be made clear, and the understanding of its importance has to be equal in both companies. Already during discussions of latter specifications a partnership oriented thinking may facilitate the process. Trust can be fostered by the fulfillment of the objectives and the application of the BSC. But in the incipience, there needs to be relied on the correctness of the other's statements, made within the BSC. In order to assure this, the buyer can attempt to put a verification mechanism at supplier's site into practice (naturally, this has to be emphasized as a support to decrease risk, not controlling, so that loss of trust is avoided).

Furthermore, the possible implementation of the Balanced Scorecard approach is confined by the general characteristics of the relationship. So, both companies have to strive for long term cooperation, since the BSC is a long term oriented approach. The short term results are given as well, but one has to be aware that there is some implementation time required, followed by a period until the first results. Another part of these relationship characteristics is the market position of both companies. In order to enable a successful implementation, both companies have to be on an equal basis for negotiations. Otherwise either the buyer would try to push the supplier to improvement to reduce management effort, or the supplier would be unwilling to put effort into improvement only for one customer, who represents only a small part of his orders and profit; briefly, there has to be partnership orientation on both sides.

Finally, the required flexibility during supplier improvement efforts has to be mentioned. The interviews found that the companies don't use a structured approach for supplier improvement. It is conducted with a high flexibility, concentrating on the issues of biggest importance (e.g. the ones found in the audit). The BSC has the advantage that it concentrates on the processes, attends to the relationship and can be adapted to the individual situation. However, since it is a structured approach, some of the flexibility is lost. There are measures, initiatives, owners and dependencies, which have to be considered before undertaking a step. Nevertheless, when planning long term cooperation respectively a partnership, with both companies profiting and from beginning approaching it on this basis, the BSC can be capable of being adapted and applied to the needs at hand.

The in the beginning stated objectives were worked out. A relationship improvement Balanced Scorecard was designed, which considers and focuses the lacking supplier's capabilities, and the different culture/strategies of buyer and supplier. The improvement components represent the critical issues that need focus and monitoring on the short term, whilst paying attention to the strategy: The monitoring embraces the measurement of short term progress with view on the long term objectives, which represent continuous relationship improvement with the stretching goal "partnership". The goal partnership symbolizes the buyer's wish to source high quality at low risk and low cost. The supplier's aim to increase his profit, which is based on efficiency and effectiveness enhancement and order growth, is facilitated as well.

Validation

In the scope of this work the validation of this Balanced Scorecard approach could not be finished. The appliance in a buyer supplier relationship in order to validate the BSC's support of improvement was due to limited time not possible. Although it is a requirement to have short term results in order to motivate the supplier, the relationship development process is not a short term activity. Correspondingly, the validation would need to regard the buyer's approaching process to the supplier, the order processing and the delivery, and afterwards to regard the continuous improvement process, in order to be meaningful.

However, when applying the designed Balanced Scorecard in a company it needs to certain extent adaptation first, in order to fit to the individual situation. Further can be stated, that many researches (e.g. /Cre-05/; /Kau-04/ and others) show that a successful application of an adapted Balanced Scorecard is possible; this fact therefore can be taken as validated. Since the strategic objectives included in the presented BSC are derived from research, which often was based on practical results, and from the interviews with companies in China, the right direction to success is supposed to be given. Limited success may result less from the BSC approach itself or from the relationship improvement considering the given strategic objectives, but rather from the limitations given above.

8 Summary and Outlook

8.1 Summary

In the past twenty years the supply chain underlay significant changes. Companies began to focus on their core competencies leading to rising outsourcing and stronger dependency on suppliers. Therefore, the supplier development and improvement gained importance and has today even strategic relevancy. Further, the globalization enables companies to shift their supply chain to countries, where production costs are lower. In order to stay globally competitive Industrialized Country (IC) mechanical engineering companies from the investment goods industry discover the possibility to outsource to low cost countries (here China) to decrease costs for their bought-in parts. Still, the shifting to Chinese suppliers is not an undertaking without drawbacks. Regularly problems with quality and delivery reliability occur. Together with high risk these factors can lead to a big shrinkage of the expected savings and even make the project fail. Consequently, the IC buyers attempt to decrease the occurrence of these issues. Supplier development and improvement emerge to be appropriate approaches on the Chinese market.

However, the known supplier development and improvement approaches lack consideration of Chinese related characteristics and don't provide an applicable framework. For this reason, this work presents the main characteristics companies have to consider when aiming for a buyer supplier relationship in China. In order to avoid the barriers and foster the elements beneficial for this relationship, an adapted Balanced Scorecard (BSC) can be applied. Besides of the relationship improvement, this approach has to enable the supplier's attainment of minimum capabilities to meet the current production requirements.

The Balanced Scorecard enables both companies to align their differing strategies in one framework. The main goal from the IC buyer is to source high quality with low risk, and with possibly high savings. Further, this company is long term oriented, since the China project requires a high effort. The supplier thereagainst strives for a high profit, often without long term strategy. As the strategic orientation and short term monitoring are basic characteristics of the BSC it is well suitable for the case at hand. Starting with the employees' culture and knowledge as basis for all processes, the BSC goes on with the cooperation perspective. Here the improvement of the relationship elements that drive a partnership oriented relationship is focused. The enhancement of these elements facilitates the advanced and joint improvement of the supplier's internal processes. This is important especially in the beginning, in order to reach a required capability level. These improvements result in direct benefits for supplier and buyer. Latter one's requirements are fixed in the following customer perspective. By fulfilling the requirements the risks are decreased for both companies. The achieved higher value of the relationship is based on increased efficiency on both sides, higher profit for the supplier and increased savings for the buyer.

The Balanced Scorecard combined with Strategy Maps enhances the understanding of improvement benefits, the communication of issues and the coordination of actions between IC buyer and Chinese supplier; these are critical factors for success. The flexibility of the BSC allows individual adaptation and application to fit a specific relationship.

8.2 Outlook

According to the survey results, the number of companies sourcing high technology products will rise in the future. The suppliers' knowledge and their capabilities are considered to rise. Nevertheless, it will take many years until the buying companies can rely on the supplier's promises as they do it in Industrialized Countries, but it seems not to be impossible. The companies are eager to learn when benefits are recognized: after understanding the issues, the product quality and delivery reliability can increase strongly, was found by the interviews. The best results were made with strong involvement by the buyer, explaining the issues and agreeing on plans. This fact is supported by the presented Balanced Scorecard. Its transparency and logic can lead to mutual understanding and trust. Once the applied method yields fruits the relationship is enhanced and can grow steadily. However, the supplier's understanding, as a critical element for the BSC to work, lacks confirmation. Future research should verify the applicability and understand ability of the BSC when a buyer tries to explain the aim and the benefits of the BSC to the supplier. It is required to consider that the language still can be a barrier (even with interpreters).

However, a validation to prove the BSC functioning was not conducted. The included strategic objectives and the measures were derived from the interview findings; possible initiatives for improvement were created but there is no prove for functionality. So, it is desired to apply this Balanced Scorecard with strategy maps in a real developing relationship between IC buyer and Chinese supplier. Practical results from the industry may show the applicability regarding the defined objectives, measures, and initiatives; a following transformation and adaptation may lead to a superior scorecard. This may be also reached by further research in this area. Room for research is further given by the fact that for this work only buyers in China were considered; this creates a one-view-perception on the problems. It would be useful to find out about the suppliers' wishes and problems directly from supplying companies, in order to enhance the scorecard regarding their culture, understanding of relationships and problems. Furthermore, the consideration of the organizational and informational capital was not discussed in this approach, as some other aspects of the companies and their relationship. On the one hand these are important factors, on the other hand these elements were not essential for the improvement approach; room for future research is given herewith.

The Chinese market will probably rise steadily in the future. Companies, which don't source from China yet, will have to do this step in order to stay globally competitive. The mass production industry is today followed by the specialized industry with low order volumes. Therefore, the problems discussed have to be approached and solved thoroughly; a structured proceeding is inevitable. Consequently, future research has to focus the emerging risks and the quality and delivery, as they are the main requirements from buyer's side and hence are responsible for the supplier's profit. Existing approaches will require adaptation to the Chinese specialties.

Further, the connection possibility of the Relationship Improvement Balanced Scorecard into existing company BSC should be analyzed, since the fifth perspective might cause adaptation problems.

A. References

[App-05]   Appelfeller, W., Buchholz, W.: "Supplier Relationship Management: Strategie, Organisation, und IT des modernen Beschaffungsmanagements". Wiesbaden: Gabler, 2005

[Arv-98]   Arveson, P.: "What is the Balanced Scorecard?". http://www.balancedscorecard.org (visited 20.08.2006), 1998

[BSC-06]   Balanced Scorecard Collaborative, http://www.bscol.com, 26.07.2006

[Cre-05]   Creelman, J., Makhijani, N.: "Mastering Business in Asia – Succeeding with the balanced scorecard". Singapore: John Wiley & Sons (Asia), 2005

[CSC-06]   Council of Supply Chain Management Professionals, http://www.cscmp.org, 26.07.2006

[Dun-04]   Dunn, S. C., Young, R. R.: "Supplier Assistance Within Supplier Development Initiatives". The Journal of Supply Chain Management: A Global Review of Purchasing and Supply, Volume 40, Number 3, pp. 19-29, Institute for Supply Management, August 2004 (http://www.ism.ws, 15.12.2005)

[Fle-06]   Fleischer, J., Wawerla, M., Schlipf, M., Vodicka, M.: "Risk Assessment of Low-Cost Suppliers". 22nd Industrial Marketing and Purchasing Group Conference, Milan, 7-9 September, 2006

[For-99]   Forker, L. B., Ruch, W. A., Hershauer, J. C.: "Examining Supplier Improvement Efforts from Both Sides". The Journal of Supply Chain Management: A Global Review of Purchasing and Supply, Volume 35, Number 3, pp. 40-50. Institute for Supply Management, August 1999 (http://www.ism.ws, 15.12.2005)

[Gro-06]   Groenewald, H.: „Bindung lokaler Fuehrungskraefte in China". p. 46-48; PERSONAL - Issue 06/2006

[Han-99]   Handfield, R. B.: "Going Global". Praxis – Best Practices in Purchasing and Supply Chain Management - by CAPS, p. 9, Volume 2, issue 1, Center for Advanced Purchasing Studies, September 1998, (http://www.capsresearch.org, 15.12.2005)

[Han-00]   Handfield, R. B., Krause, D. R., Scannell, T. V., Monczka, R. M.: "Avoid the Pitfalls in Supplier Development". Sloan Management Review; Massachusetts Institute of Technology, Volume 41, Number 2, Winter 2000

[Han-02]   Handfield, R. B., Nichols, E. L. Jr.: "Supply Chain Redesign. Transforming Supply Chains into Integrated Value Systems". Upper Saddle River: Financial Times Prentice Hall, 2002

[Har-97]   Hartley, J., Jones, G.: "Process Oriented Supplier Development: Building the Capability for Change". International Journal of Purchasing Materials Management, summer 1997 (http://www.ism.ws/ResourceArticles/1997/ /jsum974.cfm, 15.12.2005)

[Had-04]   Harding, M.: "Which form of supply chain management will work best for you?". 89th Annual International Supply Management Conference, April 2004

[Har-04]	Hartmann, H.: "Lieferantenmanagement: Gestaltungsfelder, Methoden, Instrumente mit Beispielen aus der Praxis". Hartmann, H. (Hrsg.); Gernsbach: Deutscher Betriebswirte-Verlag, 2004
[Hu-05]	Hu, Kang Gang: "China – Strategien im Wettbewerb. Deutsche Perfektion versus Chinesische Dynamik" Presentation at the Conference of the Staufen Akademie, 06.12.2005
[Jeh-02]	Jehle, E., Stuellenberg,, et seq., Schule im Hove, A.: "Netzwerk-Balanced Scorecard als Instrument des Supply Chain Controlling". Supply Chain Management, Sonderdruck aus IV/2002 (http://www.ipm-scm.de/IPM-SCM_Archiv/SCM_2002_IV_Jehle.pdf, 20.05.2006)
[Kap-04]	Kaplan, R., Norton, D.: "Strategy Maps – Converting intangible assets into tangible outcomes". Summaries.com, 2004 (www.summaries.com, 05.05.2006)
[Kau-04]	Kaufmann, L.: „X-BSC – Measuring the Performance of truly strategic supplier relationships". Practix – Good Practices in Purchasing and Supply Chain Management, Volume 7, Center for Advanced Purchasing Studies, March 2004 (http://www.capsresearch.org, 20.05.2006)
[Kau-05]	Kaufmann, L., Panhans, D., Poovan, D., Sobotka, B.: "China Champions. Wie deutsche Unternehmen den Standort China für ihre globale Strategie nutzen". Wiesbaden: Gabler, 2005
[Kra-95]	Krause, D. R.: "Supplier Development: Expectations vs. Results". NAPM 80th Annual International Conference Proceedings, Anaheim, California Arizona State University, Tempe, May 21, 1995 (http://www.ism.ws, 15.12.2005)
[Kra-99]	Krause, D. R., Handfield, R. B.: "Developing a World-Class Supply Base". Focus study by CAPS, Center for Advanced Purchasing Studies, 1999 (http://www.capsresearch.org, 15.12.2005)
[Kro-98]	Krokowski, W.: "Globalisierung des Einkaufs: Leitfaden für den internationalen Einkäufer". Krokowski, W. (Hrsg.); Berlin; Heidelberg: Springer-Verlag, 1998
[Las-06]	Laschke, A.: "SCM und Balanced Scorecard". (http://www.competence-site.de, 20.05.2006) helbing management consulting, 2006
[Min-98]	Min, Hokey: "A World-Class Supplier Quality Control Program". Praxis – Best Practices in Purchasing and Supply Chain Management - by CAPS, p. 1, Volume 1, issue 3, Center for Advanced Purchasing Studies, March 1998, (http://www.capsresearch.org, 15.12.2005)
[Nee-04]	Neef, D.: „The supply chain imperative: how to ensure ethical behaviour in your global suppliers". New York: Amacom, 2004
[Ogd-04]	Ogden, J. A., McCarter, M. W.: "Better Buyer-Supplier Relationships through Supply Base Reduction and Supplier Performance Measurement". Practix – Good Practices in Purchasing and Supply Chain Management, Volume 8, Center for Ad-

vanced Purchasing Studies, December 2004 (http://www.capsresearch.org, 15.12.2005)

[Pat-00] Patterson, J. L., Amann, K. M.: "Strategic Sourcing: A Systematic Approach to Supplier Evaluation, Selection, and Development". Practix – Best Practices in Purchasing and Supply Chain Management, p. 1, Volume 4, issue 1, Center for Advanced Purchasing Studies, September 2000 (http://www.capsresearch.org, 15.12.2005)

[Rug-06] Ruggiero, S.: "Performance Measures in the Supply Chain". (www.unicatt.it/convegno/UC-LSE/paper/Ruggiero.pdf, 26.07.2006) 2006

[Sal-05] Salmi, A.: "Managing supplier relations in Western purchasing from China". Published in "Proceedings of the 14th IPSERA Conference: Researches in purchasing and supply management". IPSERA 2005 Conference, 20-23 March 2005, Archamps, France; IPSERA (Institute of Purchasing and Supply Education and Research Association), 2005

[Sat-05] Sattler, R.: "China – Strategien im Wettbewerb. Deutsche Perfektion versus Chinesische Dynamik" Presentation at the Conference of the Staufen Akademie, 06.12.2005

[Soe-99] Soellner,, et seq. N., Mackrodt, C.: "Leadership Practices in Procurement Management: Procurement—Creator of Value, Driver of Business Strategy". in "Handbuch Industrielles Beschaffungsmanagement" Hahn, D., Kaufmann, L. (Hrsg.); S. 75-99; Wiesbaden: Gabler Verlag, 1999

[Ter-94] Terenzini, P. T., Borden, V. M., Banta, T. W.: "Using Performance Indicators to guide strategic decision making". Terenzini, P. T (editor-in-chief); San Francisco: Jossey-Bass Publishers, 1994

[Von-99] Vonderembse, M. A., Tracey, M.: "The Impact of Supplier Selection Criteria and Supplier Involvement on Manufacturing Performance". The Journal of Supply Chain Management: A Global Review of Purchasing and Supply, Vol. 35, No. 3, p. 33, Summer 1999 (http://www.ism.ws, 15.12.2005)

[Wag-03] Wagner, S. M.: "Intensity and Managerial Scope of Supplier Integration". The Journal of Supply Chain Management: A Global Review of Purchasing and Supply, Volume 39, Number 4, pp. 4-15. Institute for Supply Management, November 2003 (http://www.ism.ws, 15.12.2005)

[Wag-06] Wagner, A.L.: "Guideline for the Assessment of Chinese Suppliers in global production". Diploma thesis No. PRO – 0119, Institute for Productions-Science, University of Karlsruhe, 2006.

[Wat-93] Watts, C. A., Hahn, C. K.: "Supplier Development Programs: An Empirical Analysis", International Journal of Purchasing and Materials Management, pp. 11-17, April 1, 1993 (http://www.ism.ws, 15.12.2005)

[Wil-95] Wilson, S. R.: "Beyond quality: an agenda for improving manufacturing capabilities in developing countries". Vermont: Edward Elgar, 1995

Annex

The Balanced Scorecard for Buyer Supplier Relationship Improvement

The Balanced Scorecard for Buyer Supplier Relationship Improvement - Theme A
(illustratively with exemplary figures)

Strategic Theme		Balanced Scorecard			Action Plan	
Perspective & Strategy	Objective	Measures	Target / Status		Initiative	Owner / Budget
Financial — Productivity strategy: Increase efficiency (S), decrease SMgt.effort (B)	No intervention required during the order processing	• Rework rate • Delayed problem announcements • Positive milestone reporting • Repetitions of mistakes	0/o 0.1/o. 0.8 1/p	0.3 1/o. 0.2 3/p.	• o = orders • d = days • hr. = hours • 0.xx = percent	
Customer — "Open-Channel" for bothsided-feedback	Every critical department to have a particular communication partner	• Delayed problems-reporting due to missing communication link • Ratio unstable processes / standardized processes (sheets)	0.2 0/0.2	0.6 1/4	• Align a concrete communication partner at the supplier's site to a manager at the buyer's site • Order processing milestones are consulted with buyer • Develop easily applicable sheets	
Internal — Communication distances and TIME reduction	Employees to know exactly where to report problems and feedback	• Time for feedback to take • Required time of involvement to receive a successful supply. Involvement Time Single Audit Deficits/ Overall time (B) • Lead time	1 hr 5 hr x d	9 hr 7 hr. x d	• Enhance efficiency of involvement • Reduce the Single Deficits requiring most of the time • Compare Lead times to competitors and upon that motivate improvement (or make suggestions)	
Cooperation — Competitive Partnership orientation	Make the relationship advanced in comparison to other relationships in China	• Planning and realizing new orders/ order volumes • Innovation-suggestions from supplier's side • Number of suggestions not order-related suggestions/questions/co operations • Number of personal meetings / order	1/1 2/p. 2/p. 3/o.	0/1 0/p. 0/p. 8/o.	• Enhance competencies and foster trust by sharing future plans • Reward suggestions, penalty on actions on one's own account if impact on buyer's order • Make schedule in forefront (trust)	
Learning & Growth — Purchasing manager + Improvement team close relationship with supplier	Collegial co operation between supplier's employees and improvement team and procurement manager	• Response time for claims /[Las-06] p 5/ buyer • Response time for claims /[Las-06] p 5/ supplier • Average problem solving time	4 hr. 4 hr. 1 d.	8 hr. 17 hr. 3 d.	• Motivate both side's employees that this has a high priority • Foster understanding by arranging employee exchange, joint activities, and workshops	

The Balanced Scorecard for Buyer Supplier Relationship Improvement - Theme B

Strategic Theme		Balanced Scorecard			Action Plan	
Perspective & Strategy	Objective	Measures	Target / Status	Initiative	Owner / Budget
Financial — Productivity strategy: Increase efficiency (S), decrease S-Mgt. effort (B)	Increased orders with lower or the same management effort	• Required workforce hours to manage order (buyer) • Ratio Caused Costs / Order cost	hr./o. $ / $	• r = rate • rep. = report on readiness	
Customer — Decrease Volatility of Product Characteristics	Reach for stable quality and delivery in time based on stable processes	• Problems occurring in suppliers procurement during order processing • Development of rework rate (triggered by buyer or by supplier) • Development of delayed delivery	x r, r. dd.	• 2nd and 3rd tier supplier visits (A, B suppliers) • Enhance the supplier's bought-in parts control • Enhance process monitoring by employing more people or asking for more feedback	
Internal — Operational monitoring of suppliers processes (QDP+risk)	Uncover inefficiency causes impacting the product characteristics, reach "German" level on the long term	• Found inefficiencies • Wasted time (no value added) • Quality gates efficiency (found/not found)	x hr. x/x	• Cost structure analysis • TQM • Apply "buyer's approaches" • Standardization of processes • Responsibilities for processes requiring improvement	
Cooperation — Stimulating "mutually-beneficial" actions (WinWin)	Fostering Win-Win by executing both side beneficial actions	• Number of strategic co operations • Ordering process time • Given bonus: quality rate or delivery in time improved to foregoing order	x hr., d. $/o. $/o.	• Strategic purchasing cooperation, etc. • Create trust by questioning for advice • Increase bonus pool	
Learning & Growth — Understand the WHY of the improvements and strive for it (S): approach correctly — not dictating (B)	Follow a mutual strategy, therefore facilitate understanding and appreciation of improvements	• Ratio Number of buyer involvement / number of supplier's problems • Dedication of supplier's employees in improvement process	x/x rep.	• Visualize direct loss of profit • Create feeling for long-term thinking • Vote employee of the month based on active involvement	

The Balanced Scorecard for Buyer Supplier Relationship Improvement - Theme C

Strategic Theme		Balanced Scorecard			Action Plan	
Perspective & Strategy	Objective	Measures	Target / Status	Initiative	Owner / Budget
Financial — Growth strategy / Increase profit (S) and savings (B)	Increase both savings and profit (decrease of risk for both companies)	• Savings in comparison to (standardized) German price • Profit/ Turnover ratio in comparison to last order(s)	% %		
Customer — Quality, Delivery in time, and price meeting requirements	Competitive products in China	• Quality rate (to German) / price (to German) to last order • Quality complaints • Delivery in time	% % %	• Reduce differences between "IC" processes and supplier's ones • Production process according to product – plans fulfilled • When decreasing involvement also decrease the price (share of profit/effort)	
Internal — Improve Supplier's Capabilities: Purchg., Production, QM (QDP+risk)	Short term Improvement of critical capabilities, decreasing major risks and gaps, assure successful supply	• Specific improvement components not in time with current improvement schedule • Risk decrease • Capabilities increase • Rework rate	x % % %	• Short term meetings and increase of active involvement • Establish quality checkpoints • Postpone order to avoid bad parts delivery • Apply Audit BSC	
Cooperation — Stimulating "mutually-beneficial" actions (WinWin)	Corrective actions and changes consider both companies benefits	• Number of actions from supplier's side detrimental for buyer (B side for S) • Give bonus: quality rate //delivery/ improved compared to last order	x $	• When changing proceedings inform the buyer about changes regularly (list) (S) • Stronger changes are to be consulted with the accordant communication partner • Incentives when obvious improvement	
Learning & Growth — Understand the WHY of the improvements and strive for it (S); approach correctly – not dictating (B)	Possible efficient improvement through inducement and motivation of supplier's management and employees	• Competency profile for buyer (S) (competencies in relationship-management, in discussing technical problems/ issues, culture) • Competency profile for supplier (B)	% %	• Buyer to enhance his level of consultancy competency by e.g. schooling • Education of supplier's employees, approached by buyer's personnel	

The Balanced Scorecard for Buyer Supplier Relationship Improvement - Theme D

Strategic Theme		Balanced Scorecard			Action Plan	
Perspective & Strategy	Objective	Measures	Target / Status		Initiative	Owner / Budget
Financial — Growth strategy: Increase profit (S) and savings (B)	Further outsourcing to this reliable supplier in order to concentrate on core competencies	• Overall savings • Paid bonuses due satisfying orders	% $			
Customer — Best value Chinese supplier (lowest cost & highest reliability)	Comparable performance as a typical German supplier at lower costs than typical Chinese supplier	• Ratio Chinese/ German supplier's performance (standard measurement) • Ratio supplier's price in comparison to other supplier's offers (both Chinese) • Risk in comparison to other suppliers	% % %		• New orders when service is reliable and fast • Stronger Involvement • Cost analysis • Assess critical departments regularly and give targets	
Internal — Know about "all" risks emerging that may have impact on supplier's business and/or the buyer	Holistic risk-management (supplier's business and impact on buyer)	• Problems occurring, which could have been avoided in forefront: Unmanaged Risks (supplier's side) • Unmanaged on buyer's side • Not reported on supplier's side	x x x		• Product processes Risk Assessment (both supplier and buyer) • Feedback from production-employees and support • Cause for non-detection of risk, avoid next time	
Cooperation — Actively stabilize and grow the cooperation	Personal contacts "friends" to bind the co operations and foster further enhancements	• Supplier's trust into long term relationship • Buyer's trust into long term relationship • Joint investments • Learn to know people (Guanxi)	rep. rep. x x/p.		• Partnership contracts • Strategic reasoning with short- and long term benefits • Involvement/ Training of employees • Cultural activities/meetings key responsibilities	
Learning & Growth — Consolidate knowledge and create lasting usability	Assure durable knowledge to save resources, decrease risk and increase efficiency	• Key staff retention (/Kap-D4/ p. 8) rate • Standards procedures and key processes having at least 2 supplier's employees involved	%/p. rep. x/x		• Carrier programs • Bonuses and raise of salary • Company culture • Log on improvements • Spread knowledge, always include two employees	

Annex

The Audit Balanced Scorecard

AUDIT Balanced Scorecard

Perspective & Strategy	Strategic Theme	Objective	Measures	Target / Status	Action Plan - Initiative	Owner / Budget
Financial	Increase orders (S+B) and attain a nonrisky fulfillment of supply	Decrease of risk leads to increase of savings, increase of orders, efficiency and incentives leads to increased profit	• Risk decrease amount/ percent / period (B) • Orders delivered not in time / in time • Rework number/ total order number	$,% x/x %		
Customer	Fulfill Quality and Delivery; monitor the progress of improvement	Concurrent monitoring and intervention to assure the achievement of a stable supply	• Quality/Delivery positive reporting ratio during processing (x is / x should) • Quality complaints after delivery or late delivery • Defects caused by known problems • Occurring "known problems" • Occurring new problems	x/x x x x x	• Optimize the feedback, personal contact, questioning • Concentrate more on the current monitoring (e.g. "feedback-gates" in product processing) • Enhance lastingness by standardisation and 0-mistake-approaches • Anonymous identification and reporting of problems, higher incentives	

Internal	Learn about and execute actions against deficits	Lasting improvement through learning, executing and changing (S)	• Improvement Components
			   o Audit Results
			   o Risks
			   o Product
			• Not executed improvements at due date (ratio) in risks, audit, and product
				%
				%, $
				x
					• Find solutions for decreasing the single gaps, risks and defect products, beginning with the critical ones
					• The reasoning must be supported by approaches	

Cooperation	Share knowledge of problems as well as knowledge of solutions	Sharing knowledge as basis for partnership – enable it	• Number of suggestions from buyer's side • Ratio of realized suggestions / suggestions from buyer's side	x x/x	• Enable cross-functional involvement → solution, feedback • Reasoning has to follow supplier's strategy (e.g. short-term profit)	
Learning & Growth	Employees are basis – foster culture, WHY-understanding	Supplier's management and employees to be convinced of the improvement – they are the basis	• Supplier's employees to report issues and problems (everybody has to participate): Ratio of taken opportunities/participants • Number of bonuses paid or number of suggestions made	x/x x	• E.g. online tool where problems can be anonymously described – to be done by every employee once a week • Bonuses have to be a certain % of saved money and be increased by the amount taken	

IX